Japanese Flower Arrangement
Notebook

JAPANESE
FLOWER ARRANGEMENT
NOTEBOOK

Patricia Kroh

MILTON B. FREUDENHEIM, SR.
CHIEF PHOTOGRAPHER OF
AUTHOR'S FLOWER DESIGNS

DOUBLEDAY & COMPANY, INC.
GARDEN CITY, NEW YORK
1962

FIRST EDITION

LIBRARY OF CONGRESS CATALOG CARD NUMBER 62–7396
COPYRIGHT © 1962 BY PATRICIA KROH FREUDENHEIM

Dedicated
to
my son and daughter
Milton and Diane

Foreword

Patricia Kroh is a sincere admirer of the culture of my country, and as will be obvious to the readers of this book, she has pursued the study of Japanese flower arrangement with enthusiasm, zeal, and perseverance. Miss Kroh has rightly understood that flower arrangement in Japan is an art and not merely a technique or a pretty facet of an exotic (to Western minds, perhaps) civilization; it is instinctive for us, who are profoundly conscious of our natural surroundings, to express profoundly Japanese values and concepts through an artistic use and re-creation of nature and nature's objects.

A worthy service to Japanese culture has been performed by Miss Kroh in this endeavor to penetrate and explain what often abounds in paradoxes—the motivating philosophy, intellect, and feeling behind the symbols represented in the *ikebana* and in the *ikebana* tradition itself. I am sure that after reading this book, those Western lovers of *ikebana* will gain a heightened pleasure in arranging flowers and that their efforts to capture the essence of Japanese *ikebana* will take on an added dimension and beauty.

Dr. Koto Matsudaira

Ambassador from Japan to the United Nations
New York, March 14, 1961

Acknowledgments

Writing a book of this kind would be an impossible task without the friendly cooperation of many people. I am deeply grateful to those who played a part in making every facet of *Japanese Flower Arrangement Notebook* possible.

All of the new flower-arrangement photography in color and black and white is the work of my talented and devoted husband, Milton B. Freudenheim, Sr. The Japanese Consulate's office in New York made contact with members of the Tokyo Chapter of the Ikebana International Society in Japan. Mrs. George Kramer, the president, Mrs. Erwin Meller, Mrs. Reijiro Hattori and Mrs. Yoichi Hiraoka (who acted as my interpreter) in Tokyo, smoothed the way for me, and helped make my stay comfortable and interesting. The object of the Ikebana International Society is to spread interest in and better understanding of Japan throughout the world, through its culture.

It would have been very difficult for me to learn about the Japanese country, the people, and their philosophy without the warm and friendly interest of Mr. Reikichi Yokohama, Mr. and Mrs. Kenzie Kimie Hayashi, Mrs. Hazel Gorham, Dr. Chikao Fujisawa, Dr. Toru Matsumoto, Mr. and Mrs. Kei Nagashima, Mr. Jack Dagel, and Miss Eiko Yuasa.

Although my garden has been the source for most of the flowering material used in my photographs, Albert Parrella's Dahlia Garden, "Flowers by Lilyan," and the Larchmont Nurseries provided me with flowers and branches during the winter months. The interesting illustrations of Japanese gardens were furnished by the Japan Tourist Association of New York and Tokyo. Mr. Kaizo Sekido of the New York office was especially helpful.

Special appreciation goes to my teachers: Mrs. T. Usuda, Mrs. Hoga Fujiwara, Mrs. Seiti Taguchi, Mr. Sofu Teshigahara, and Mr. Isshin Mori.

The completion of a project like this depends on the loyalty and devotion of friends like Mrs. Kenneth Leonard, Mrs. Clifford G. Barnie, and Mr. and Mrs. Ken Suzuki.

Finally, my sincere and profound appreciation to Dr. Koto Matsudaira, whose approval I value most highly.

Contents

Color Illustrations

Black and White Illustrations

Introduction

Writing one chapter on Japanese flower arrangement is like being asked to give a five-minute talk covering the history of the United States. Yet that is what I had the temerity to do in my book *Design with Flowers, Unlimited.* Happily for me, the chapter called "Design with Flowers East and West" was so well received that some readers have said they would like more about my Japanese studies.

With apologies, then, to my Japanese teachers, and a low bow of recognition to the masters in the many hundreds of schools of the ancient culture and art of *ikebana* in Japan, I would like a further opportunity to tell a little more in detail about my experiences and observations in learning the techniques in the four schools of flower arrangement in which I studied.

This book is not intended to compete with the beautiful Japanese text books written by the masters of *ikebana* in Japan in their respective schools. I kept a pretty complete notebook when I was studying flower arrangement in Japan. If you follow each lesson as I describe it to you, it is my thought that you will learn to "do it yourself,"—at least until you can take that trip to Japan.

The Ikenobo and Enshu schools have always represented, to me, typical classical schools that have been popular with the Japanese people for centuries. Mr. Sofu Teshigahara, master of the Sogetsu school, and Mr. Houn Ohara, third-generation master of the Ohara school, represent the *avant-garde* in the modern trends felt in the art of *ikebana* as well as all other art forms in Japan today. As this is being written I am sure there are many new masters interpreting *ikebana* in their own way, and creating new schools in Japan, just as each teacher of painting here offers his interpretation of individual technique to his students.

There are a few other reasons for this book. When I returned from Japan, where I lived long enough to become sensitive to the attitudes of the Japanese people toward *ikebana*, I became very conscious of the confusion of ideas retained by sincere and interested students of Japanese *ikebana* in the United States. I hope to explain away some of these misunderstandings or, at least give food for thought concerning them.

There have been many questions concerning the relationship between Japanese *ikebana* and the religious philosophy of the Japanese people. What has *ikebana* to do with the Tea Ceremony? How is the Japanese garden designed to relate to the symbols that are a part of all the culture of Japan? What is the role of these symbols in the Tea Ceremony?

Japanese flower art can be a pretty superficial thing unless you have the answers to these questions. I have tried as simply and briefly as possible to answer some of them. I hope my answers will whet your appetite to read further on this profound subject. Only by understanding can we do justice to this ancient and beautiful art of Japan.

Part One
PHILOSOPHY
WITH FLOWERS

生
花
の
厂
史
と
哲
学

Lo, with delight and pride untold
I too drive in a nail of gold
To rear a Pantheon the plan
Of which at history's dawn began.

KUSA NO YUME
Gohsho yori tsukuri itonamu dendo ni
Ware mo kogane no kugi hitotsu utsu.
By Yosano Akiko

Figure 1a *The ancient music
of the koto is very popular.*

Figure 1b *Japanese men playing samasen.*

CHAPTER I

History

There is something romantic and beautiful about the history of *ikebana,* the special art of arranging flowers that has been a distinctive cultural rite of Japan for more than thirteen hundred years. *Ikebana* dates so far back in the history of Japan that the earliest records come from ancient stories told in picture form, *Man-yo-shu* (poetry), philosophic writings, and information passed down by word of mouth from generation to generation. As early as the sixth century the Japanese were a people with a keen awareness of the beauty of nature and a philosophy that required that they demonstrate this appreciation.

When Buddhist priests came to Japan by way of Korea in the sixth century, they brought with them the ritual of placing floral offerings in the shrines and temples as a part of the Buddhist belief in preserving plant life. These plants and flowers were placed there as symbols. They were not offerings made in the manner with which we associate Japanese flower arrangement today. They were simple bunches of branches and flowers placed in urns called *bukkwa.*

There is a story I read long ago about the samurai (warriors of ancient Japan), A.D. 1007, who returned from battle, set aside their swords and garments of war, retired to their gardens, and arranged branches and flowers as they contemplated and meditated on the beauty before them. This simple act refreshed the spirit and cleansed the mind of evil thoughts. The beauty of this picture, like a lovely Japanese print, remained with me through the years. When I finally traveled to Kyoto in Japan, I was amazed to find the settings for my picture still standing. Many of the beautiful ancient gardens, temples, and shrines were there. Even the Golden Pavilion, where the Tea Ceremony (*Cha-no-yu*) and flower arrangement (*ikebana*) of the fourteenth century were performed, remains. (Plate 1.)

The ancient cultural rite of *ikebana* is still a part of life in Japan. The Japanese people hold fast to tradition. The ancient music of the *koto* (a large, harp-like instrument) and *samasen* (an instrument like a mandolin) is very popular. (Fig. 1a–b.) Young women enjoy and learn the beautiful and graceful movements of the ancient dance. Noh plays (classical drama) are performed in the same manner they have been for centuries, with an all-male cast. The lovely kimonos worn by men, women, and children are cut by very much the same pattern and worn in the same way they were centuries ago. (Plate 2.) The kimono is still considered the proper dress for all important occasions. This does not mean that the Japanese taste for modern ideas in music and dress and even flower arranging has not advanced with the times. When I was shopping for *koto* and *samasen* recordings in Tokyo, I found a tremendous interest in Western symphonic music and American jazz. The teen-age crowd love "rock-a-billy," their name for some of our modern popular jazz. The teen-agers dress very much as our youngsters do, in sweaters, skirts, blue jeans, bobby socks, and loafers. In spite of this Western influence there is a conscious pride, even among the young Japanese, of their traditions and cultures. They all seem to know about *ikebana*.

Children wear kimonos on their festival days. There is a wonderful custom of all the boys of a certain age group, e.g., six to nine years, or all the girls three to six years, celebrating their birthdays on the same day of the month, called a Festival Day.

I was in Tokyo in October during a festival for young boys in the prefecture (district) in which I lived. I could hear the beat of the drums and the music of the wooden flute from my window. I went to see what was going on and found the children having a gay time.

For those who love history, it might be especially interesting to trace the development of the art of flower arranging in Japan with the introduction of Buddhism into the life of the nation. Each era, namely, the Heian Period, 794–1191; Kamakura Period, 1192–1333; Muromachi Period, 1338–1573; Momoyama Period, 1590–1602; Edo Period, 1603–1867 (Early Edo Period, 1603–1703; a Middle Edo Period, 1716–1789; and a Late Edo Period, 1790–1867) offers proof of the importance given to the Tea Ceremony and the flower offering that was a part of this ritual.

Ikenobo is the name of the first school of flower arrangement in Japan. It had its origin in Kyoto which was the capital and home of the Imperial Palace in early history. The school was originated to teach the Tea Ceremony and the flower ceremony connected with it. Not all of the people were considered educated enough to take part in these rituals. So, in the beginning, it was really a school reserved for the clergy and nobility.

In the year A.D. 607, during the Sui Dynasty, Emperor Bidatsu sent his son, the Prince Regent Shotoku Taishi, to China. The Prince was so interested in his studies there that he went back twice so that he might learn more. Chinese civilization was quite advanced and the Emperor of Japan wished to improve the government of his country. He also wished to learn the formulas for making beautiful potteries, porcelains, bronzes, and other crafts for which the Chinese were famous. Shotoku learned much about Buddhism while he was abroad. He also learned about the delightful gardens that were a characteristic part of the Chinese scene.

When Shotoku returned to Japan from his travels abroad, he designed a temple called the Rokkakudo (Hexagonal Hall). He planned a garden and a lake beside it. Shotoku retired to this garden to live a simple life and to teach Buddhism to his people. His nephew, Ono-no-Imoko, was appointed flower master of the temple. He was in charge of caring for the flowers and making the flower arrangements. When Shotoku died, Ono-no-Imoko grieved for him and became a monk. He shaved his head and lived in a small hut by the lake in the garden. Buddhist followers came from miles around to learn his way of arranging the flowers and performing the *Chan-no-yu* (Tea Ceremony). When the students returned to their homes they would say they had been taught by "the monk who lived by the lake." In Japanese, one of the translations of the word "Ikenobo" is "place by the lake." It was not long before people were identifying their teachings with the name "Ikenobo." Their offerings, they said, were made in the "Ikenobo Way."

Ono-no-Imoko took the name of Senmu and all of his descendents have adopted the custom of retaining the syllable "Sen" in their name. Since then, Senmu Ikenobo's descendents have been the Head Masters of the Ikenobo School. The title passed from father to son, from generation to generation.

(Ono-no-Imoko) or Senmu
                    Senno
                    Senshu
                    Senwa
                    Sensho
                    Sensho
                    Senso
                    Senmei
                    Sensho
                    Senei
                    Sensei
                    Senkei   d.1039 aet.71
                    Senryo
                    Sensei
                    Sengen
                    Senkaku
                    Senrai
                    Senson
                    Sensho
                    Senju
                    Senrin
                    Senki
                    Senpu
                    Senrin
                    Seni
                    Senjun[1]
                    Senchin[2]
                    Seno
                    Senson
                    Senei
                    Senko[3]   perfected *rikkwa*
                    Sencho
                    Senson   Okanishi Hachibei went to
                    Senyo   Edo as expert to Tokugawa
                    Senko   Shogun.
                    Senjun
                    Seni
                    Senjun
                    Senko
                    Sentei
                    Semmei
                    Sensho
                    Senkei

[1] Established styles of *rikkwa, suna-no-mono* and *kiebana*. 1472.
[2] Received title of Master of the Way of Flowers from Ashikaga Shogun.
[3] Flourished 1596–1614.

There were no written rules for arranging flowers until the twelfth master, Senkei Ikenobo. He is given credit for writing the first rules regulating the method of placing flowers before the shrines. He died in 1039 at the age of seventy-one. This early style, called *rikkwa*, was placed in bronze urns in the temples. They contained large, tree-like branches, flowering shrubs, grasses, and flowers and were supposed to duplicate a natural scenic effect. The tree branch called *shin* was the tallest and it represented the distant view.

The shrub branches that were shorter were called *soe* and represented the intermediate view. The smaller flowers were called *tai* and were usually placed in a group of three representing the close view. This style of floral arrangement was used in the temples for hundreds of years. Today in Japan there is a revival of interest in the ancient *rikkwa* method of flower arranging and there are many teachers who have exhibitions showing their skill in this old Ikenobo "formal" style.

While I was in Japan I was fortunate to attend an *ikebana* exhibition and see an elderly flower *sensei* (teacher) dismantle his *rikkwa* arrangement that had been on display. It was very interesting to see how he kept the heavy tree branches in place as he removed them from their bronze vase. Sections of bamboo and grasses held together with wire served as a holder. (Fig. 2.)

Figure 2 *Holder for* rikkwa ikebana (*bamboo and grasses*).

There is a formal style of *rikkwa* (Fig. 3), an intermediate style of *rikkwa* (Fig. 4) made with more fluid lines, and an informal style of *rikkwa*, made in a low bronze dish similar to those later used for the *moribana*-style arrangements. (Fig. 5.)

About the time of the Rennaissance in Europe, the latter part of the fifteenth century, there was a decided Western influence felt in the East. This was during the reign of Yoshimasa (1436–

Figure 3 *There is a formal style of* rikkwa.

Figure 4 *An intermediate style of* rikkwa *is made with more fluid lines.*

Figure 5 *An informal style of* rikkwa *is usually constructed in a low dish.*

1490), eighth Shogun of the Ashikaga Dynasty who was a patron of the arts. He abdicated his throne in order to devote all of his time to the ceremonials and rites of Buddhism. It was he who thought the floral offerings could be made more beautiful and worthy of their important place in the shrines and temples. He commissioned Saomi, a celebrated artist and friend of his, to create an artistic pattern to be used for arrangements of plants and flowers that would incorporate the three elements of Heaven, Man, and Earth (*shin, soe,* and *tai*) whose relationship Japanese philosophy teaches and Japanese flower arrangements illustrate. (Fig. 6.) The twenty-seventh tea master was Senshin Ikenobo. Yoshimasa gave him the title of Master Kwado-no-on-lamoto (Master of the Way of Flowers).

In the seventeenth century Sencho, the thirty-second master of the Ikenobo House, was ordered by the Emperor Mizuo to hold a display of his flower art in the Imperial Palace. The Emperor was so pleased with his work that he presented Sencho with a green curtain and a flower vase and stand. These have since been adopted

Figure 6 *The three elements of Heaven, Man, and Earth (shin, soe, and tai) whose relationship a Japanese flower arrangement illustrates.*

as the characteristic distinction of the head masters of the Ikenobo school, and are presented to their most distinguished pupils.

The House of Ikenobo was organized along feudal lines with a *karo* (council) and a *jun-karo* (junior council). They form a staff of the most able flower masters with the approval of the head master. There are others who make up the Flower Cabinet, who teach, supervise, organize, and go about the country giving lectures and holding meetings and examinations.

There are fascinating legends about the House of Ikenobo. A translation that I found comes from the book by A. L. Sadler on *The Art of Flower Arrangement in Japan: "Senkei Ikenobo, Abbot of the Rokkakudo Temple, was so devoted to flowers that he roamed the hills and valleys around the capital in Kyoto in order to better study their habits and growth. He thought nothing of traveling for miles through the rugged country, and was so absorbed in his work he would even forget to eat. The Kwannon (Goddess) of the Temple was so pleased with his enthusiasm, she vouchsafed him a revelation in a dream in which she showed him all the secret lore about the arrangement of flowers and plants."* This legend was written by Kyoto Meisho Zue.

The certificate given me after my studies in the Ikenobo School in Tokyo was signed and has the seal of the young master, Senei Ikenobo, who is a direct descendant of Senmu, the first tea master in A.D. 607.

For hundreds of years the Ikenobo House reigned as masters in the Tea Ceremony and the art of arranging flowers. It was not until the seventeenth century that disciples of the Ikenobo way with flowers started making changes in the original old style. One of these first to break away was Enshu Kobori. His new method was called the Enshu *Ryu.* He had received his training under one of the leading tea masters of the Ashikaga Dynasty, Shuko Furuta Oribe. The Enshu method was supposed to be more acceptable to those who were interested in arranging flowers for decoration as well as for the Tea Ceremony. The method taught was a more exaggerated manipulation of branches and flowers that obtained a dramatic effect. Branches were cut to fit into a slot-like support and the main stems were given slightly different names. (Fig. 34.)

Although there are many stories about the origin of the

methods of arranging flowers that departed from the original Ikenobo way, they all agree on the trinity of Heaven, Man, and Earth.

It is often repeated that the tea masters lived to a very old age.
The reason for this is said to be due to their "calmness of mind,
creative interests, and tranquillity of spirit." Could it be that our
tremendous interest in Japanese flower arranging today is due to
our need for a therapy that will bring us the peace of mind and
serenity of spirit that seems to characterize Japanese flower artists,
even today?

CHAPTER II

Philosophy

Arranging flowers in the Japanese way becomes more meaningful when the philosophy on which the art is based is understood. I have always been inquisitive about the reason for the development of *ikebana* as a serious Japanese cultural rite and I went to Japan determined to learn how their philosophy was applied to this special art. At first I inquired of Western people who had lived in Japan for many years. Most of them said they had never been conscious of any special philosophical significance placed on their *ikebana* lessons. This did not satisfy me, however, and as time passed I had the good fortune to meet Japanese people in many branches of society from whom I learned that ancient Eastern philosophy and *ikebana* still play an important role in the life of most of the people of Japan, even today.

I felt reassured after speaking to Mr. Senkei Kuwabara, head master of the Kuwabara Ryu School of Kyoto. I had a very interesting visit with him one evening and through my interpreter, Miss Eiko Yuasa, who worked at the City Hall in Kyoto, I learned that the philosophical significance of *ikebana* was still very much in existence.

My visit with Mr. Kuwabara was especially memorable. When we arrived at his home we were greeted in the foyer by Mr. Kuwabara and his wife and teen-aged daughter. The daughter, who was quite tall for her age, had a very short, elfin-like hair cut and wore a long-sleeved slipover sweater, pleated skirt, bobby socks, and loafers. Her mother was dressed in the traditional Japanese kimono. Mr. Kuwabara invited us upstairs to his studio, part of which contained three Western-style chairs and a table. The rest of the area was Japanese-style (straw matting on floor) and was

Plate 1   The Golden Pavilion and many of the beautiful ancient gardens, temples, and shrines were still there in Kyoto.

Plate 2   The lovely kimono is cut by the same pattern and worn in the same way it was centuries ago. Kroh-San with her Japanese teachers and friends in the garden at the International House in Tokyo.

Plate 3   An Ikenobo arrangement in a brass hanging crescent moon of Thunbergia vine and fern is a popular style.

Plate 4   Barberry and chrysanthemums are arranged to illustrate the Ikenobo moribana style: (1) shin, (2) soe, (3) tai.

Plate 5   The Arthur Godfrey
dahlias and dried palm are
a striking example of the
nageire style in the Ikenobo
method: (1) shin, (2) soe,
(3) tai.

Plate 6   An arrangement of
ilex and rubrum lilies in
the Enshu Ryu: (1) shin, (2)
gyo, (3) otoshi.

Plate 7   A windswept arrangement of Taxus and chrysanthemums made during the month of October in Tokyo: (1) shin, (2) gyo, (3) otoshi.

Plate 8   Baptisia requires no manipulating. Its natural curves combine well with the blossom of the lily: (1) shin, (2) gyo, (3) otoshi.

equipped with beautiful old flower containers for his pupils to use. As we discussed the basic philosophy expressed in terms of flowers, Mrs. Kuwabara watched over our comfort. She brought large pottery hibachis filled with red-hot charcoal which took the chill off the cool October evening. She served delicious green tea and very special sweet cakes.

A most significant incident was the sound of very modern Western-style music accompanied by the voice of the young Miss Kuwabara, who was quite unconscious of the fact that she could be heard by us on the floor above. The modern jazz music was in sharp contrast to our serious discussion, but it typified to me the youth of Japan today.

Mr. Kuwabara was quite impressed with the interest I had in Japanese *ikebana* and philosophy. He made a very fine arrangement of aspidistra leaves which he demonstrated with the grace and finesse of a master. After making the arrangement, he executed a drawing of it and put his signature on it in Japanese. (Fig. 7.)

The books I had read described the introduction of flower arrangement to Japan well enough, but they rarely gave much space to the philosophy on which it was based. I wanted to know *why* the main branches of a Japanese flower arrangement were called Heaven, Man, and Earth, and what this had to do with the belief of the Japanese people. My questions seemed relatively simple, but to learn the answers I found myself deep in ancient Eastern philosophies—Taoism, Confucianism, Mahayana Buddhism, Shintoism, and Zen. It is from these roots that Zen-Buddhism stems and these are the philosophies that inspired the Japanese "way of life." *Ikebana*, I learned, was only one of the symbolic Japanese cultural rites.

TAOISM

My first research was in Taoism (*Tao Te Ching: The Book of the Way and Its Virtue*) by the famous Lao-Tze. For a while I wondered what this might have to do with Japanese flower art until I came to the axiom that stated, "Man and the World form fundamental unity," and later on, "Heaven, Man, and Earth are the three principal planes of philosophic thought." In another part of this wonderful little book I read, "Just as the work of man

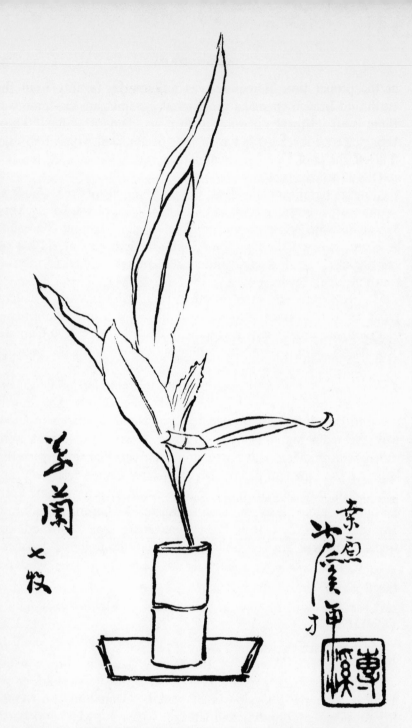

Figure 7 *Master Senkei Kuwabara of the Kuwabara Ryu of Kyoto made an arrangement of aspidistra leaves in the classical style and drew a picture of it for me.*

at the proper time is required, as well as the fertility from the earth and heaven to make the harvest possible, in the same way there is an intimate relationship in every domain of life." These thoughts were recorded in China approximately in the year 300 B.C. This was a period of very high intellectual activity in China.

Other Taoist theories claimed: "The earth is square; on it heaven is placed as a cover, supported by pillars at the four points of the compass. The sun, the moon, and the planets move in their respective courses." That course is called "Tao" (the Way). There is the Tao of Heaven that corresponds to the Tao of Earth and the Tao of Man.

All phenomena work in certain categories expressed by a symbol of numbers according to the Taoist theory: the five elements (fire, water, wood, metal, and earth), the five points of the compass (counting the middle of the center also), the five seasons of the year (counting the middle of the year separately), the five planets, the five colors, the five tastes, and the five musical notes. Tao is full of mysticism and superstitions.

CONFUCIANISM

The Chinese are by nature a practical people and much of Taoism was difficult for them to follow wholeheartedly. It was natural then that they should be receptive to the interpretations of the practical philosophy of Confucius. Confucius emphasized the importance of the development of the mind. He gave the Taoist concept of Virtue a moral meaning. Taoism taught the negative approach to Virtue, the idea that it is only by making the mind a compete blank and performing no act of either good or evil that the soul of man remains pure. Confucius gave man a moral code (the Golden Rule). He preached the doctrine of "Universal Love"—first, "filial piety," the love and duty of a child to his parents, and then love of others.

There were no floral offerings made to the gods in the Chinese temples at this period, but there were regular offerings of sheep, cattle, grains, fruits, and branches of trees. It was customary to place food near the tablets of one's ancestors, even though they were deceased, in accord with the idea of filial piety. Rice and other foods placed in the temples indicated a wish for further blessings from the gods who could make it possible.

Confucius did not advocate "meditation" as a means of purifying the mind as did the Taoists. He considered "meditation" a waste of time and believed in a positive approach to an ethical life. His books of rules for a good life, as well as his sayings have been an important part of Eastern philosophies for hundreds of years.

BUDDHISM

I learned that the first Buddha was a young man born in India about 560 B.C. His family was from a region at the foot of the Himalaya Mountains a hundred miles north from Benares on the border of Nepal. His name was Siddhartha of the Gautama family. His ancestors were warriors and his grandfather was a nobleman of the tribe. It seems unusual that a young man (twenty-nine years old), married, with a family, should wander off from his village, leaving all worldly goods behind, to seek the answers of life and death. But according to the translations from the Hindu records, there was corruption in the church of the Brahmans of India and people were eager for a change.

One day as Siddhartha sat beneath a fig tree, the legend goes, he had a dream. In the dream the answers to the mysteries of life and death he was seeking were revealed to him. From that time on he was known as the Buddha (Enlightened Seer), who had won the perfect peace of "spiritual knowledge" (Nirvana).

The traditional Indian creed is based on the belief that the universe is inhabited by a countless number of souls in varying degrees of elevation. Each passes through an endless number of births and deaths in a great variety of bodies. Every moment of experience that each soul undergoes in each incarnation is the direct result of an act performed in a former life. These acts were supposed to bear fruit in a future experience. This could be a long line of sorrows and might not give the poor Hindu much to look forward to.

The new philosophy taught by the young Buddha was a "middle path." He denied that there is a continuous subject of thought in the individual. He taught the "selflessness" of man. There is no "I am," the new teacher said. He wrote the book of the Four Noble

Truths on which all Buddhism is based. According to Siddhartha's teachings there is no permanent "self" and there is no real "matter." "Man emerges from cosmic space in ignorance, develops as an individual, with weaknesses of the spirit, potentialities of love and hatred, name and form and finally, disease, sorrow and death overtake him." Nirvana could only be earned by those who attained a "way of enlightenment" which meant a life of the Golden Rule and the Noble Truths.

ZEN BUDDHISM

It was a thousand years after the death of the first Buddha (A.D. 6) that Bodhi-Dharma, the twenty-eighth Buddha, came from India to China. There were two major schools of Buddhism at this time, the Mahayana and the Hinayana. The Hinayana was a more orthodox concept. It did not recognize the constant change in the universe in its relationship to man and the earth. The more modern school, called Mahayana, not only recognized the constant change, but also the need for enlightenment, and the importance of passing on the torch of enlightenment to others.

Bodhi-Dharma, who was called the Blue-Eyed Monk, was founder of Zen Buddhism. Zen has more than one translation. It may be interpreted as meaning "meditation." It also means "concentration of mind." And still a third translation is "enlightenment of mind." Zen was founded on many Chinese and Indian philosophies. From Taoism Zen gained some of the supernatural in relating man to Heaven and Earth. Zen adopted the ethical and moral teachings of Confucius, the moral code that emphasized that man should live to arrive at the life of enlightenment that would assure him Nirvana.

SHINTOISM

The Japanese had a philosophy of their own, called Shintoism (the Way of the Gods), when Zen Buddhism was brought to Japan. To make Buddhism acceptable to the Japanese, it was necessary for the Chinese monks to blend the Shinto and Buddhist ideas together. Shinto national gods became Buddhist saints, and in the eighth and ninth centuries the religion was called the "twofold way of the gods." Buddhist idols and relics found their way into Shinto temples and shrines.

The Shinto deities are chiefly gods of nature and natural forces. At the head is the Goddess of the Sun. Of minor importance are the Moon God and Star God. There is a God of Rain and Thunder, a Goddess of Food and Crops, a God of Mountains and Trees, and a God of Fire. Besides, there are gods who were once men— rulers, heroes, or men prominent in arts. The Shinto worship of ancestors and human deities has been attributed to the Chinese Buddhist influence.

There are still many adherents of Shintoism in Japan. When I was there I had a very interesting visit with one of the foremost professors of the Shinto philosophy, Dr. Chikao Fujisawa. I remember well our conversation concerning my quest for the relationship of modern Japanese *ikebana* with the Japanese philosophy of Zen. Dr. Fujisawa said, "Shintoism is the basis of all interest in flower arrangement." He also said, "Man was born out of the womb of Mother Nature," and that "Shinto and the Sun Goddess are synonymous." He mentioned the familiar association of *yo* with "expansion" and the word *in* with "contraction." He spoke of the "unity beneath the diversity of nature." The Shinto theory is that of a permanent center represented by the sun, with constant change and "mutations without." Again I heard the words "Heaven, Man, and Earth" and their relationship. He also spoke of "tranquillity and serenity" in association with the beauty of nature and suggested that we would all enjoy a better way of life if we took example from nature in its relationship to Heaven, Man, and Earth.

I interpreted this to mean that man's final peace after life comes only when his relationship to life on earth has had a virtuous course.

CHAPTER III

Cha-no-yu

HISTORY OF TEA

Tea was known in Japan before the Kamakura era (1185 to 1388). The Zen monk, Eisai, brought tea seeds from China and had them planted in a monastery garden. Minamoto Sanetomos (1192 to 1219) the Shogun of that time, was ill. Tea was supposed to have medicinal value and Eisai brought it with a book he had written on tea to the Shogun as a gift. There was no record of the Tea Ceremony as it was practiced in China until the Zen monk, Dai-o, returned to Japan in 1267. It was during the reign of Yoshimasa at the time of the Ashikaga dynasty that the ceremony was developed artistically.

The famous tea master, Rikyu, contributed many ideas that made the *Cha-no-yu* as we know it today. Japanese say, "Tea keeps the mind fresh and vigilant," and that it "symbolizes Buddhism."

CHA-NO-YU (TEA CEREMONY)

The Japanese people who perform the *Cha-no-yu* usually are sensitive to the deep philosophical significance attached to the many details of this beautiful ceremony. Those who have had a sound cultural background are better able to perform "the Tea," as it is often called. Occidentals who are invited to witness and participate in this ancient Zen Buddhist ritual without an explanation of what "the Tea" represents, miss the point of it all. To them it may appear to be "much ado about nothing."

There are books written about the tea cult of Japan with notes of explanation. A particularly noteworthy one by Mr. Okakura Kakuzo states: "Teaism is a cult founded on the adora-

Figure 8 *The simple interior of the tearoom does not distract from the beauty of the* kakemono *or* ikebana.

Figure 9 *The tiny entrance way to the teahouse is intended to bring humility to all who crawl in.*

Figure 10 *Cleanliness is practically a law for those participating in the Cha-no-yu. The stone water basin in the garden is adjacent to the tearoom with a dipper made of bamboo for rinsing the mouth and hands before entering.*

tion of the beautiful among the sordid facts of everyday existence." We could stop with this explanation and have a clue
to the basic meaning of the entire Cha-no-yu. The author goes
on: "It [the Tea Ceremony] inculcates purity and harmony, the
mystery of mutual charity and the romanticism of the social
order. It is essentially a worship of the imperfect, as it is a tender
attempt to accomplish something beautiful in this impossible
thing we know is life." It is the desire to bring even more beauty
to the ritual of "the Tea" that the Japanese made a simple flower
arrangement a part of it.

THE CEREMONY

When observing the Cha-no-yu or participating in it, one
should keep in mind that this rite was not originally intended to
be a social amusement in Japan. Many serious acts of piety are
represented in this simple ritual. The proper deportment is one of
respect, humility, and silence, which gives the small tearoom a
churchlike atmosphere.

The physical requirements for the performance of the Cha-no-
yu are quite interesting. The tearoom in a Japanese house or a
separate teahouse on the grounds, is of very simple structure. If
it is a part of the house, the room is often measured by the
number of tatamis (straw mats). A mat is 3 feet wide and 6 feet
long. The average tearoom contains four and a half tatamis or
about 10 square feet. There is a tokonoma (alcove) in the room
and little furniture or decoration other than the kakemono (scroll
painting) and later the ikebana. (Fig. 8.) If it is a separate building, the roof is often thatched of straw and the doorway through
which the guests enter is a small opening just large enough to
crawl through on hands and knees. (Fig. 9.)

Only about five at a time may be present in the tearoom. They
sit quietly on their knees waiting for the tea master or hostess,
who arrives after all the guests are present. There is generally an
opening in the floor for a brazier where the water kettle is heated.
The ceremony is sometimes performed in front of the tokonoma.
The reason for the very simple surroundings for the performance
of "the Tea" is very important. There should be no distractions
from the ceremony itself and the beauty of the scroll and the

Figure 11a *The tea implements consist of the tea caddy, a waste bowl, the tea bowl, a measuring instrument of bamboo for spooning out the green powdered tea, and a bamboo beater.*

Figure 11b *The teacup is passed around after the tea is brewed.*

flower arrangement. One must bear in mind that the humblest and plainest objects contain something to be admired. Even beauty of sound is suggested by the water bubbling in the kettle. This sound reminds one of the wind blowing through the pine trees. The tiny entrance way is intended to bring humility to all who enter, for in the tearoom there is no class distinction. The wealthy and poor alike, the nobleman and peasant perform "the Tea" together.

Two most important utensils in the performance of the Tea Ceremony are the *cha-ire* (tea caddy), and the *chawan* (tea bowl). Many thousands of yen have often been paid to obtain an old tea caddy that may seem to have no beauty to the average eye, but because of its long historical background becomes a treasure. It may be many centuries old with cracks and mends, possibly the work of a famous tea master. Those who are fortunate may inherit a tea bowl and other implements for the performance of "the Tea" that belonged in their family.

Cleanliness is practically a "law" for those participating in the *Cha-no-yu*. To help make cleanliness possible, there is generally a *tsukubai* (stone water basin) (Fig. 10) filled with water in the *roji* (garden) adjacent to the tearoom with a dipper made of bamboo for rinsing the mouth and hands before entering. Of course, the *zori* (shoes) are left outside.

No one has a chance to be bored during the *Cha-no-yu*. There is always the beauty of the *kakemono* (scroll painting) to be appreciated. Never have I seen such silent, thoughtful appreciation of beauty as I did during the *Cha-no-yu*. The flower arrangement is often not made until the second part of the ceremony is performed. The tea master, or host, who acts as the master of ceremonies, brings the tea implements with him when he enters the room. They consist of the tea *cha-ire* (caddy), a *koboshi* (waste bowl), the *chawan* (tea bowl), and a measuring instrument of bamboo for spooning out the *chashaku* (green powdered tea). (Fig. 11.) It is customary for each implement to be admired before the tea is prepared. The teacup is passed around, also the tea caddy and it is with the greatest care that these utensils are handled. They should never be picked up high to be admired, but are kept close to the *tatami*. Upon first receiving the article the participant bows low from his kneeling position as it is placed before him. He then examines it carefully on all sides and passes it on to the participant on his left. The tea brew is then prepared. First the small napkin that was tucked into the *obi* of the tea master is placed in the right hand and wrapped around the fingers in such a way that it is compact and easy to use. Then the top of the tea caddy is wiped with deft, graceful movements. The teacup is washed with boiling water and then the green powder is placed in it. A Japanese teacup has no handle.

The tea is brewed by pouring boiling water on the green powder tea and beating it thoroughly with a *chasen* (small bamboo whisk). It forms a consistency very much like cream of spinach soup. The brew is passed first to the person on the left of the tea master who places the cup before him, bows low, takes the cup in both hands with one hand under the cup, using it like a saucer, as he tastes it. The cup is then passed to the person on the left, who turns the cup clockwise and sips a little of the brew, bowing low before doing so.

Sometimes a special sweet cake that looks like a bun, with a doughlike substance on the outside and a sweet filling that tastes like honey, ground almonds, and sweet potato, is served. (I did not get the recipe, so this is only a guess from the taste.) The bun is eaten with care and placed between bites on a small paper doily that the participant is expected to bring with him. When the tea master gives the signal, all the guests bow out of the tearoom, leaving by the entrance they came through.

There is generally a place to sit where the garden may be viewed, called the *roji* (garden courtyard or waiting place). Here the dripping water through the bamboo pipe as it spills into the stone water basin joins with the pleasant sound of the birds. If the garden has been well designed, each object has special significance connected with the appreciation of nature and simple beauty. The guardian stone, trees, shrubs, stone lantern, pool, steppingstones, all are designed to show the relationship of man to the universe.

One learns the lesson of humility through the grandeur of a tree that stands in the distance. The garden teaches the lesson of the constancy of a sun, moon, and stars in the Heaven and their relationship to Earth and Man. The succession of bloom is a lesson of life as we view the bud, the half-opened flower, full-blown

Figure 12 *An arrangement of poppies in different stages of development (bud, full-blown, and seed pod) symbolizes the constancy of
nature.*

flower, and the seed pod in a flowering shrub. A flower arrangement may repeat this simple story of nature's constancy. (Fig. 12.)

The classical schools of *ikebana* teach the use of plant material
that represents the correct relationship of trees and shrubs and
flowers. Tree branches are usually used as the tallest, with shrubs
relatively shorter and flowers usually representing earth, with the
shortest stems in the arrangement. Even a dead branch covered
with moss or lichens is appreciated in a Japanese flower arrangement. Often the dramatization of life is expressed in sharp contrasts of a gnarled root and a single delicate blossom. (Fig. 13.)
The Eastern philosophies teach that there is a *yo* and *in* in all
phases of life and they indicate this by the use of light and dark,
coarse and delicate, rough and smooth, sunny and shady, in their
flower arrangements, gardens, and other cultural arts.

Figure 13 *Japanese* ikebana *portrays the sharp contrasts of yo and in, in an arrangement of a single delicate camellia in a gnarled root.*

After the participants in the Tea Ceremony have a chance to sit in the *roji* in order to appreciate the beauty of the garden, a gong or bell is sounded to invite them to return. By this time the tea master has added the flower arrangement to the *tokonoma*. As the guests return they bow low before the *tokonoma* to show their respect for and appreciation of the beauty before them. They sit quietly, taking in what they see.

Mr. Daisetz T. Suzuki, in chapter VIII of his book *Zen and Japanese Culture*, states: *The art of Tea is most intimately connected with Zen, not only in its practical development, but principally in the development of the spirit that runs through the ceremony itself. The spirit in terms of feeling consists of 'harmony' (wa), 'reverence' (kei), 'purity' (sei) and 'tranquillity' (jaku). These four elements are needed to bring the art [Tea Ceremony] to a successful end. They are all the constituents of a brotherly and orderly life.*

Part Two

KROH SAN GOES TO SCHOOL

諸宗派に学ぶ

Spring's mild caresses
The gnarled old plum tree waits not.
Beneath the snow flakes,
With all their beauty hidden
It thrusts its buds out boldly.

ANONYMOUS

from *The Art of Flower Arrangement*
by A. L. Sadler

Figure 14 *The shoji screen in my Japanese-style room in Tokyo made an artistic background for an Ikenobo arrangement of pine and lilies.*

CHAPTER IV

Getting Started

WHY STUDY IN FOUR SCHOOLS?

What is there about the way they arrange flowers in Japan that is different from the way we do it? What is the special quality that is characteristic of Japanese *ikebana*? What is the philosophy so often mentioned on which the art of *ikebana* is based? These are the questions that I went to Japan to have answered.

I had decided to learn the flower art of Japan first hand and to do this I selected not one but four of the hundreds of schools in Japan in which to study. I chose the Ikenobo method because it was the most ancient, and the Enshu because I had studied this beautiful classical school in the United States many years ago. The Ohara and Sogetsu are both popular modern schools and were highly recommended for their fine staff of teachers and head masters. It was a wonderful experience. Japan is like no other place in the world and I am full of superlatives about the Japanese teachers who went all out to assist me to learn as much as possible about their *ikebana*. (Plate 2.) When I was introduced to a Japanese person they would say "Kroh San is *ikebana sensei* (teacher) in United States." I would hurry to explain, "Not Japanese *ikebana sensei*, Western-style." A Western *ikebana sensei* was a novelty. "Is *ikebana* so popular in the United States?" they would ask.

ATTITUDE

I had read about Eastern philosophy before visiting Japan, but it would have been helpful if I had studied the language also. It is much better to communicate directly.

The Tea Ceremony and the attitude of the people toward their *ikebana* was of particular interest to me. What I found is well worth repeating: "The spirit in terms of feeling consists of 'harmony,' 'reverence,' 'purity,' and 'tranquillity.' These are the four elements necessary to bring the art to a successful end." The Japanese character "wa" means "gentleness of spirit" as well as harmony. The attitude of "reverence," "gentleness of spirit," and "tranquillity" is one I became aware of while I was studying *ikebana* in Japan. I was conscious of this spirit in my instructors while they were arranging the branches and flowers during my lessons and I noticed it in the manner with which Japanese people generally view *ikebana*. Often they would fall to their knees and bow very low before the *tokonoma* when they entered the home of a friend. My room was always filled with many flower arrangements from each lesson. Whenever Japanese visitors arrived they gave each arrangement a special kind of thoughtful consideration. They never criticized or expressed preference for one or the other. They would just admire and often say *"kirei,"* the word for "pretty" in Japanese. When a Western visitor lives in Japan for any length of time, contact with gentleness, reverence, and tranquillity is bound to rub off a little. When I arrived in Tokyo I was tired, a little nervous, and impatient to get started with my lessons. The pleasant, unhurried way of doing things soon took over and I found myself relaxed and getting more joy out of flower arranging than I ever had before.

COMPETITION

There is nothing competitive about flower arranging in Japan. Large flower exhibitions are held in the leading department stores. They provide special space for these shows that attract thousands of viewers. The shows are not judged, but only the best *ikebana* *senseis* are invited to exhibit, each in his own school. It is very much like an exhibition of paintings or sculpture. Often paintings are shown in a room adjoining the one in which the *ikebana* is on display.

I was invited to attend a flower show at the Ohara school one day. It was a show in which all the advanced students who wished to get "teaching certificates" exhibited. Each vase was identical, as was the plant material. All the arrangements were made in the *nageire* (throw in) style. The three masters who judged each arrangement passed from one to the other and considered them individually. There was no competitive judging.

LIVING JAPANESE STYLE

I lived Japanese style while studying in Tokyo. This means living in a *tatami* room, the name given a room with a straw matting. The *futon* (bedding) is put away in a special cupboard during the day, and there is very little furniture in the room. The International House where I stayed was a large modern building, but even here they had a "Japanese-style" room. The room had a small *lanai* (porch) that overlooked a beautifully designed Japanese garden. There were *shojis* (sliding panels), sliding glass doors, and screens between the room and the *lanai*. The *shojis* made an artistic background for flower arrangements. (Fig. 14.)

A low, black lacquer table had a place of honor in front of the *shojis*. An alcove with a window seat, a low table for my typewriter, and two rattan chairs was all the furniture in the room. A chest of drawers in a walk-in closet was hidden from view by sliding doors.

When the days were warm and humid, I had *ikebana* lessons on the *lanai* overlooking the garden. It was an inspiring experience to learn the fascinating ancient and modern techniques of *ikebana* in this charmed atmosphere.

Figure 15 *The Ikenobo containers are usually very simple in design. An arrangement of gladioli in a traditional Ikenobo container.*

CHAPTER V

Ikenobo School

Mrs. Usuda was my *sensei* in the Ikenobo school. She was a pleasant-looking little Japanese lady with a warm, friendly manner, who spoke no English. It was necessary to have an English-speaking Japanese friend act as interpreter. She had been a student in the Ohara school, and was extremely interested in her first introduction to lessons in one of the oldest classical schools of Japanese flower arrangement. I had a small electric water kettle that I had brought with me from home and each day after Mrs. Usuda arrived, I would make tea and we would drink it sitting on our knees, Japanese style, before starting the day's lessons.

Mrs. Usuda brought beautiful old bronze and bamboo receptacles for me to work in and ordered branches and flowering material suitable for the Ikenobo style of flower arrangement. The receptacles were sturdy and simple of line with little or no ornamentation. (Fig. 15.)

The Ikenobo method of teaching advocates using the natural bend of branches. (Fig. 16a–d.) This method tries to duplicate nature as nearly as possible in the way branches and flowers are arranged. For example, the *shin*, or Heaven branch, *soe*, Man, and *tai*, Earth, if composed of trees, shrubs, and flowers in an arrangement, would be placed in a position relative to their height in nature. Therefore, in an arrangement of pine branches, andromeda, and iris, the pine would represent the *shin*, or Heaven branch, andromeda the *soe*, or Man branch, and the iris would represent the *tai*, or Earth group. (Fig. 16d.)

For one of my first lessons Mrs. Usuda brought a straight bamboo cylinder flower container. "*Migi-bana* means right-handed

Figure 16 A moribana *arrangement of pine (for the distant view),
andromeda (for the intermediate view), and iris (for the close view)
is characteristic of the Ikenobo way:* (1) shin, (2) soe, (3) tai.

Figure 17   A migi-bana *of yellow Supreme marigolds in a bamboo
container*: (1) shin, (2) soe, (3) tai.

flower arrangement," she said, "and *hidari-bana* means left-handed flower arrangement. One imagines the sun shining from either the right or left side drawing the blooms and leaves toward it." (Fig. 17.)

While the Ikenobo school teaches the recognition of the natural curve of a branch or flower, it also teaches the expert manipulation of branches and flowers to improve the effect. Bending a branch is done slowly and with great care. Both hands are used to support the branch on the underside with pressure exerted from above by the two thumbs. (Fig. 18a–e.)

After learning the words *migi* and *hidari* I was taught the word *kubari*. This means "holder" or "support." The *kubari* is easily made from a thick branch of wood. The wood selected for this purpose must be supple (rose of Sharon, viburnum, or willow). The piece Mrs. Usuda selected was about three fourths of an inch thick. It was straight and clean of all branches. I was taught to measure across the top of the vase and cut the branch a trifle longer than was necessary. (Fig. 19a–e.) Two small notches are cut at each side of the branch two-thirds across. With deftness and care the branch is split in the middle to the point of the two notches. There it is bent back to form a "Y."

To fit the *kubari* into the top of the bamboo vase I whittled away small amounts of the wood until it was a tight fit. This simple type of holder makes a fine support. The stems and branches are often placed so that the ends rest against the side of the vase. In fact, it is a good idea to cut the end of the stems at an angle to make them fit more securely. (Fig. 20.) A supple piece of wood about half an inch thick called a *tomeki* is used to hold the stems in place after the flowers are arranged in the *kubari*. (Fig. 19e.)

Shin is the name the Ikenobo school calls the main or Heaven branch. It is cut about two and one half times the height of the vase. The secondary line called *soe* or Man, is cut two thirds the length of the *shin* branch. The third line, *tai*, is cut one third the length of the *shin* branch. If *shin* and *soe* are branches from a tree or shrub, *tai* is often composed of flowers. *Tai* may be a unit of three blooms and is placed in the *kubari* tilted forward facing the viewer. A shorter bloom, called *tani*, which means "valley," is placed directly in back of *tai*, and directly in back of that is a

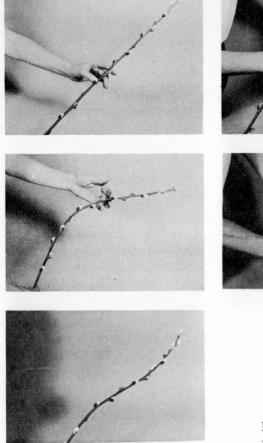
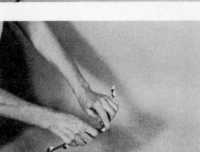

Figure 18 *It is not difficult to bend a branch.*

flower slightly shorter than *tai* called *doe*, which means "hillside." There are other stems called *mai*, which means "filler." They are placed in front and in back of the main branches to support and fill out the design, giving it depth and perspective. The placement of the *mai* branches allows for personal taste. (Fig. 21.)

I was taught to try each branch in the *kubari*, remove it, and then arrange the flowers in my left hand, one directly in back of the other so they could be placed in the holder in the proper sequence cut at the right length. All the stems are tilted slightly at an angle as they leave the *kubari*. The *shin* branch is the tallest and strongest, with its tip over the center of the arrangement. There is a traditional manner in which the branches are placed in an Ikenobo arrangement. (Fig. 22.)

Figure 19   *The kubari is an important part of a successful Ikenobo arrangement.*

Figure 21 *Willow and chrysanthemums are great favorites for classical* Ikebana: (1) shin, (2) soe, (3) tai.

Figure 20 *If you cut the stems at an angle, they will rest against the side of a vase.*

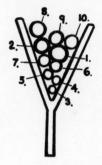

Figure 22 *There is a traditional position of stems in the* kubari *for the Ikenobo school:* (1) shin, (2) soe, (3) tai, (4) tani, (5) doe, (6) mai, (7) mai, (8) soe-oku, (9) ushiro, (10) mai.

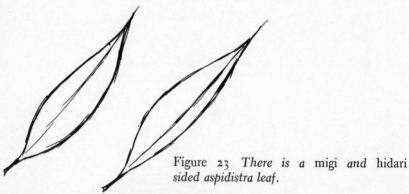

Figure 23 *There is a* migi *and* hidari *sided aspidistra leaf.*

Flowers arranged in a shallow dish *moribana* style in the Ikenobo school may use a *kenzan* (needle-point holder). The flowers are placed in very much the same relative position as they are in a kubari in *heikwa* style. Sometimes a metal disc in which a traditional Ikenobo wooden *kubari* is fitted is used for a *moribana*-style arrangement. (Fig. 16a.) (Plate 4.) The Ikenobo school has a special technique for the arrangement of aspidistra or halan leaves. There are *migi* (right-sided leaves) and *hidari* (left-sided leaves). (Fig. 23.) These are the names given to the aspidistra leaves a little wider or narrower on the side of the central vein running through the leaf. In Japan the florist separates these leaves into bundles according to whether they are *migi* or *hidari* leaves. It is difficult to find aspidistra leaves for sale at a

Figure 24 *Ikenobo niju ikebana of magnolia buds, tulips, and narcissus. If the top arrangement is large, the window arrangement is made relatively smaller:* (1) shin, (2) soe, (3) tai.

florist and most nurseries do not care to cut leaves from this old-fashioned house plant in the northeastern part of the United States, but ti and draceana foliage may be substituted. (Fig. 7.)

A *niju-ike* is a popular container for Ikenobo school arrangements. It is a bamboo cylinder with a *nado* (window) cut out. There are many variations of a *niju*. They sometimes have two or three openings. The flowers are arranged on different levels. If the top level has a cascading *shin* line and *soe* line, the *tai* group may be arranged very simply in the lower window within the confines of the opening or each level may be arranged as a unit. If the top arrangement is large, the window arrangement is made relatively small. (Fig. 24.) Sometimes only the lower window is arranged and when this is done, it usually extends out either on the right or the left side of the container and swings up to the top.

Hanging arrangements are very popular in the Ikenobo school. Mrs. Usuda taught me to make an arrangement in a bamboo hanging boat. The *shin* line cascades out of the boat like an oar. When the boat is outgoing and leaving the port, it is called a *hidari* arrangement. The incoming boat requires a *migi* arrangement. The *shin* line is measured by the length of the boat plus the depth. The *soe* line is arranged upright and must not be longer than the chain by which the boat hangs. If the *shin* and *soe* lines are branches with no flowers, the *tai* group may be composed of blooms. (Fig. 25a–b.)

Baskets are very popular as flower containers in the Ikenobo school. These baskets are often of a very fine weave and the cane is stained a dark mahogany color with a high luster. The shapes vary and with each shape a different style of arrangement may be appropriate. I found some lovely old baskets and enjoyed using them particularly for the *nageire* style of arrangement. This style is used in all of the schools of *ikebana*, I later learned. (Fig. 26.)

The word *nageire*, I was told, means "throw in." It is supposed to depict a very naturalistic arrangement of flowers or branches and flowers that seem to be "falling out" of a tall, slender vase. This is a very interesting design to construct because in doing so you learn the many different ingenious ways of making flowers stay in place without the use of commercial holders; you also learn the principles of design, namely, balance and proportion,

Plate 9   *Enshu cedar of Lebanon and chrysanthemums.*

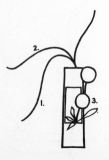

Plate 10   In the springtime branches from the Bristol red
Weigelia and pale pink single peonies provide easily arranged
flowering material for a niju ikebana in the Enshu way: (1)
shin, (2) gyo, (3) otoshi.

Plate 11 *The Enshu Ryu teaches moribana style. Clipped palmetto palm branches are easily bent and curved when they are green and arrange well for an Enshu moribana:* (1) shin, (2) gyo, (3) otoshi.

Plate 12 *Ohara slanting water-viewing moribana. Hankow willow and early tulips make a seasonal arrangement:* (1) subject, (2) secondary, (3) object

Plate 13   Ohara heavenly
style moribana designed
with rhubarb chard
and zinnias: (1) subject,
(2) secondary, (3) object.

Plate 14   A glass long-necked bottle provides a
lovely container, for Grape Ivy, camellia, buds, and
blossoms in the Ohara cascade nageire style: (1)
subject, (2) secondary, (3) object.

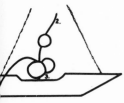

Figure 25 *When the bow of the boat is on the right as you face it, it is called an incoming boat; reversed, it is called outgoing. An arrangement of marigolds and turquoise berry vine depicts an incoming bamboo hanging boat. The arrangement of a rose with pine is outgoing:* (1) shin, (2) soe, (3) tai.

which are extremely important to the execution of a good flower arrangement in this style.

The *shin* branch in a *nageire* arrangement is the longest and strongest branch or flower stalk that cascades out from the neck of a vase in a horizontal position. This *shin* line can be made to stay in place in many ways: (1) the stem may be bent so that it rests against the side of the vase; (2) the stem may be supported by a wooden *kubari* cut like other traditional Ikenobo *kubaris* with the end of the stem cut at an angle to rest against the side of the vase; (3) a strong branch of wood may be forced to fit securely in the top part of the vase and the stem of the *shin* branch split

Figure 26   *The* nageire *style is quite appropriately arranged with maximum rhododendron branches and blossoms in the Ikenobo school:* (1) shin, (2) soe, (3) tai.

and secured against this heavy branch for support; (4) a *kenzan* (metal pin holder) can be dropped to the bottom of the vase and a strong branch placed in it. The top of the strong branch may be split so that the end of the *shin* branch is secured in it so that it leaves the top of the vase in a horizontal position without falling out. The line drawing in Figure 27 illustrates all of these methods.

The tip of the *shin* branch in a *nageire* should turn up, facing heavenward. The *soe* or Man branch is more easily secured, sometimes supported under the *shin* branch about two thirds the length of the *shin* and also with an upturned tip. *Tai* is usually composed of flowers, and their position in this case creates a balance because of the manner in which they are placed and their proportionate size. With the proper straight-sided vase, tall and slender in design, the *nageire* style of arrangement is one that may be easily learned by Western students of *ikebana*. (Plate 5.)

Some Western students confuse "style" with "school" or "method." Nageire *is not a school or method. It is a "style" of* ikebana *performed with slight variations in the individual Japanese schools of flower arrangement. This is also true of* moribana. *It is a style of* ikebana, *not a special school, and is popular with* all *the schools of* ikebana, *classical as well as modern. There may be* moribana *styles of* ikebana *as performed in the Ohara, Sogetsu, the Enshu, or the Ikenobo school.*

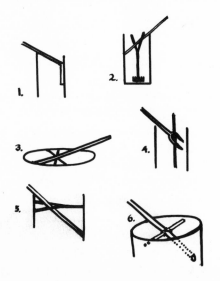

Figure 27 *There are six ways of making holders for* nageire *arrangements.*

CHAPTER VI

Enshu School

The Enshu school of flower art is another of the ancient classical schools that branched off from the Ikenobo school during the fifteenth and sixteenth centuries. Enshu Kobori was its founder. He was a disciple of the famous tea master of the Ashikaga Dynasty, Shuko Furuta Oribe. It was thought that this more exaggerated style of curving branches had an appeal to the Japanese who was not interested in *ikebana* as a part of the *Cha-no-yu*, but rather as a lovely artistic expression, with plants and flowers, for the home. (Plate 6.)

During the seventeenth and eighteenth centuries the Enshu *Ryu* (School) was very popular in Japan. The new techniques for making the branches stay in place as well as the methods for manipulating and improving the natural curves of branches and stems created a challenge that stimulated an interest in *ikebana*. Here was a technique that took even more concentration, time, and effort than some of the simpler and more naturalistic schools taught.

In the early 1930s when flower arranging as an art was just beginning in the United States, the Enshu method seemed most attractive to Western students of *ikebana*. I did not have an opportunity for very much instruction in this famous old school, but I struggled along after having a few lessons from a charming Japanese lady who lived in a nearby community to Larchmont. Because of these few lessons in the Japanese way with flowers that applied the principles of good design that I could understand, with a philosophy that I was a little vague about, I was launched in a hobby that has filled my life with beauty in many forms.

Much to my disappointment, when I reached Japan to study

ikebana, I found few teachers of the Enshu method of *ikebana* living in Tokyo. I was fortunate, however, that the teacher whose services I was able to obtain was such a fine one. He was a real artist whose hands moved deftly and quickly to produce rhythm and curves with branches that were stiff and straight. His name was Mr. Isshin Mori from Yokohama. Mr. Mori's father before him was a master of the Enshu *Ryu.* In studying the family tree of Enshu masters through the centuries I found the name Mori Issai, third in line from the school's founder, and I wondered if my teacher was a direct descendant from one of the original Enshu *Ryu* masters.

Mr. Mori spoke no English, although he seemed to understand me quite well. My first lesson was a real "do it yourself" project in making a special Enshu *kubari.* Mr. Mori came equipped with a kit containing a saw, small axe, sharp knife, and flower scissors. It was necessary to use a saw to construct the Enshu *kubari.* (Fig. 28.)

Specifications for making Enshu *kubari:*

One piece of wood (teak or cypress preferred), 12"×1"×¼"

One piece of plywood, 12"×1"×1/16"

Very fine-gauge wire (rustproof preferred)

Small saw

Sharp knife

Method: Measure the inside dimensions of the vase, and from the 1"×¼" piece cut two pieces one fourth inch larger than the exact inside measurement. For example, if the inside measures 4 inches, cut the wood 4¼". Measure and cut the 1/16" plywood also. From the 1"×¼" moulding cut four ¼" pieces. Whittle one end of each of the four pieces into a wedge. Put the pieces together, while holding them in one hand, in this order:

1. One molding, 4¼"×1"×¼".
2. One wedge at either end, with wedge side facing down.
3. Plywood, 4¼"×1"×1/16".
4. Two wedges placed at either end like first.
5. Molding, 4¼"×1"×¼".

Hold together securely in hand as you make slight indentation in wood with sharp knife all around at each end so that the wire when wrapped around will not slip. Wrap securely with very fine rustproof wire (copper or stainless steel).

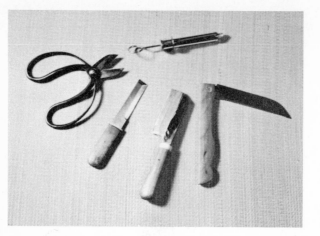

Figure 28 *Flower arrangement tools are necessary in the Enshu Ryu.*

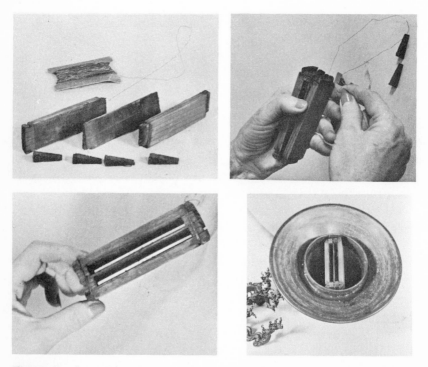

Figure 29 *Learning to make my own Enshu kubari has proven very helpful to me.*

Whittle off the ends very carefully to make tight fit. This slot type of holder can be tipped to the right or left after it is secured in the disc in the *usubata* (a bronze flower receptacle) or top of a straight-sided vase. (Fig. 29a–d.)

Later, Mr. Mori helped me select a traditional style of flower container made of bronze. Bronze containers suitable for the Enshu method I learned were generally a little more ornate and delicate in feeling than those used in the Ikenobo school. Cone shapes supported by symbolic waves or dragons and urn-shaped bronze containers supported by three delicate feet and topped by a large disc were very popular designs for receptacles made for this school. (Plate 6.)

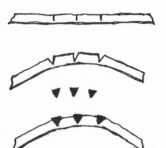

Figure 31 *There are tricks to bending a stiff branch.*

Choice of plant material is of next importance in making a traditional Enshu *ikebana*. Willow, ilex, taxus, juniper, cedar, and pine are some of the varieties that are available in the United States and are particularly suitable for the main branches of an Enshu *ikebana*.

Mr. Mori explained that the branches are selected very much as they are in the Ikenobo school. The tallest, strongest branch or flower is selected for the *shin* branch. He suggested that this branch is usually cut from two to three times the height and width of the container. When a *usubata* is placed on a small table or stand, the height of this stand is considered in deciding on the length of this *shin* branch. The *shin* branch in this case may be five times the length of the container. (Fig. 30.) The base of the branch should be straight and cleaned of its foliage. If the wood of the branch is supple, it may be bent after measuring one and a half hand spreads from the bottom. If the wood is brittle and too heavy to bend, small wedges may be cut and inserted into slits that are made in the branch at the points where the arranger wishes the branch to bend. (Fig. 31.) This is quite a trick. The wood from which the wedges are cut must be from the same tree or shrub and have the same exterior bark. When this is done artistically, it is sometimes impossible to see where the wedges have been inserted.

Often a Japanese *ikebana* depicts the season, not only by the selection of plant material, but by the design of the arrangement. It is not uncommon to see an arrangement with a wind-swept look during the months when it is especially windy in Japan. (Plate 7.)

An appreciation for driftwood that gives the appearance of a tree bare of leaves originates, I believe, with the Japanese appreciation of nature at all times of the year. Even the silhouette of a bare branch has beauty. I have found that seeking appropriate or unusual tree or shrub branches for *ikebana* has made me more aware of a quality of beauty to which I was formerly quite blind. (Fig. 32.)

Arrangements may be entirely composed of flowers (Plate 8) but generally this style calls for branches of trees and shrubs with few flowers. The *shin* branch is selected after careful examination from all sides, keeping in mind that this branch symbolizes the majesty of Heaven. It is the longest and strongest branch. It extends from the flower holder for at least four inches, straight and clean of foliage and stems. The height of the *shin* branch varies. It may depend on where the arrangement is to be placed. When an arrangement is placed on a small table fifteen or twenty inches from the floor, the height of the table and depth of container are measured. I have seen lovely Enshu arrangements made with the *shin* branch one and a half times the depth of the vase or width of a shallow dish, but more often twice or three times this height. A taller arrangement gives a more dramatic effect. (Fig. 30.)

If the branches are too tall, they may be cut down, but "Beware of cutting too short," my teacher warned me. In the beginning it may be necessary for you to whittle a little more off the ends of the branches as you prepare them to fit into the slotlike Enshu holder. After you have determined the length of the stem, the next step is pruning. By holding the branch up before you against a light background, you will make each essential and unessential

Figure 30   *The height of the small table used under a classical Japanese flower container often dictates the length of the branches and stems.*

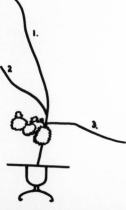

Figure 32 *Japanese flower arranging taught me to appreciate the beauty of a bare branch. An Enshu arrangement of euonymus atropurpureus branches and white azalea illustrates this:* (1) *shin,* (2) *gyo,* (3) *otoshi.*

leaf and stem stand out. With a sharp clipper cut as close to the main stem as is possible and then camouflage with a little brown oil paint or charcoal. (Fig. 33a–f.)

Next, decide whether the arrangement is to be *migi* or *hidari*. When the main branch, *shin*, is bowed to the left of the arranger as he faces it, it is called a *migi-bana*, or right-handed arrangement. The Japanese consider this as if they were standing in back of the flower arrangement. As the branch leaves the holder, it would be slightly tilted to the left for a *migi-bana*. Mr. Mori instructed me to measure with two hand spreads from the end of the branch to determine where to start the first point for bending. Gentle pressure with both hands with thumbs supporting the branch is the best method for bending. (Fig. 18.)

I learned a very interesting technique of bending and pulling the branch gently but firmly at the same time until a slight snap is heard on the inside. This is a way of breaking some of the tough fibers to allow the branch to stay as it is bent without breaking the bark on the outside. Mr. Mori used this technique of pulling and bending when he worked with taxus, cedar, and juniper, I noticed.

After the first bend is placed in the branch, the second bend makes a reverse curve with the tip facing heavenward. The second branch is called *gyo* (Man). Again two hand spreads is measured for the first bend. This branch is placed directly in back of the *shin* and is cut to measure two thirds the length of the *shin* branch. It swings a little to the left and back of the *shin* branch (for a *migi-bana*). The third branch to place is the *otoshi* (Earth). This branch is placed directly in back of *gyo*, but swings out horizontally to the main two branches toward the viewer (for a *migi-bana*). This branch varies in length, but the tip must turn up. (Plate 9.)

Supporting and filler branches and blooms may be placed next. The number of blooms and buds are really not dictated in the Enshu *Ryu*, but it is suggested that to create an effect of good design with balance and proportion, odd numbers of branches and blooms are preferable. However, when three branches are used, two blossoms are acceptable. If the blossoms have foliage on them, it is best to strip the stems about two or three inches above the water line of the arrangement. As the branches are placed one behind the other, the effect is that of a single strong stem.

Figure 33 *The classical Enshu arrangement requires time and skill.*
Take one step at a time as I did when I constructed an arrange-
ment of cedar of Lebanon branches with chrysanthemums: (1) shin,
(2) gyo, (3) otoshi. See PLATE 9.

Figure 34 *Mr. Mori's unusual Enshu arrangements sometimes combine the ancient* rikkwa *style and modern Enshu* ikebana: (1) shin, (2) gyo, (3) otoshi.

Figure 35 *An Enshu nageire-style arrangement of rhododendron branches and blossoms is well related to the simple bamboo container:* (1) shin, (2) gyo, (3) otoshi.

My teacher taught me how to construct a beautiful Enshu *ikebana* in a simple bronze cone-shaped container with taxus and chrysanthemums (Plate 7) for one of my lessons in Tokyo. You will note the interesting little trick of stripping the needles off the tip of the *shin*, *gyo*, and *otashi* branches to give the arrangement a light, graceful look.

Each flower master arranges the *niju* (two-section bamboo container) in a slightly different way. (Plate 10.) It was interesting to learn that the Enshu *moribana* style is executed very much like the arrangement made in the bronze *usubata*. An arrangement of clipped Palmetto Palm that bends very easily when green and gladioli have the *shin*, *gyo* and *nagashi* branches easily identified. (Plate 11.) Mr. Mori made many sketches in my Japanese flower-arrangement notebook to illustrate the numerous varieties of designs possible in the Enshu *Ryu*.

Figure 36   *An Enshu arrangement* heikwa *style of budding plum branches, and freesias heralds the coming spring:* (1) shin, (2) gyo, (3) otoshi.

Each day we would try another design. It was a challenge to try to duplicate the work from the long practiced hand of Mr. Mori. I could have gone on and on, always learning something new. It was toward the end of our association that Mr. Mori brought me several pictures of flower arrangements he had made for some important exhibitions in Tokyo and other parts of Japan. His work was most unusual and seemed to incorporate the ancient *rikkwa* style with the modern freedom of line. (Fig. 34.)

The Enshu interpretation of the *nageire* style is not unlike the Ikenobo way. It is made here in a bamboo cylinder with blossoming branches of rhododendron maximum to illustrate this popular style. (Fig. 35.)

The *heikwa* Enshu *ikebana* is made in a brass container of ancient Chinese design. Budding plum branches and white freesias demonstrate what can be done with a few flowers arranged in the Japanese way. (Fig. 36.)

CHAPTER VII

Ohara School

I had met Mr. Houn Ohara in New York when he was on a world tour. His *ikebana* demonstration was extremely interesting and enthusiastically received in New York. I will always remember Mr. Ohara's free-style *ikebana* for its originality and modern design.

It was Mr. Ohara's grandfather, Unshin Ohara, who founded the present school. Mr. Unshin Ohara had been an *ikebana* master who had the courage of his convictions and believed that *ikebana* designs could be constructed in receptacles other than the bronze urns used up until that time. He introduced the idea of making flower arrangements in the shallow dish called *moribana* at a large exhibition given by flower masters in 1907. Mr. Ohara and his father before him developed the *moribana* style of *ikebana* that has been adopted by every other school of flower arrangement in Japan.

The Ohara Center, as the Tokyo school is called, is a well-equipped modern building buzzing with activity day and night. The school was staffed with many fine teachers, some of whom spoke English. Mrs. Hoga Fujiwara, my Ohara *sensei*, was a pleasant little lady who helped me as quickly as possible to master the elementary basic designs that "beginning" students in the Ohara method must learn before they are permitted to work in the advanced "free style." *Moribana* arrangements are divided into five basic patterns—"upright," "slanting," "cascade," "heavenly," and "contrasting." Arrangements made in a tall vase are called *heikwa ikebana*. The *heikwa* styles are also called "upright," "slanting," "cascade," "heavenly," and "contrasting." (Fig. 37a and b.)

There are two ways of handling each of these basic styles. Mrs.

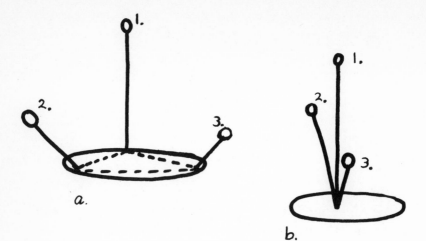

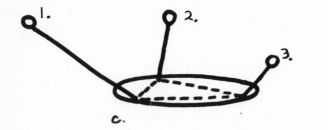

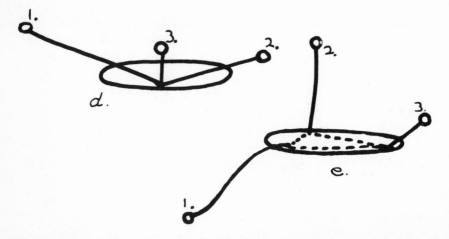

Figure 37a *There are five basic moribana-style designs in the Ohara school: (a) upright, (b) heavenly, (c) slanting, (d) contrasting, (e) cascade.*

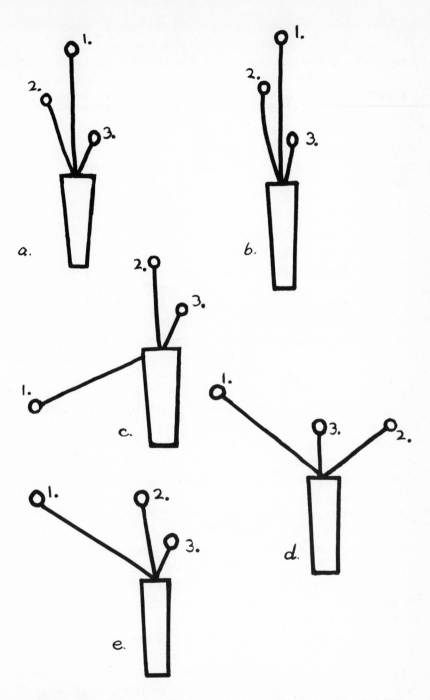

Figure 37b *There are five basic heikwa-style designs in the Ohara school: (a) upright, (b) heavenly, (c) slanting, (d) contrasting, (e) cascade.*

Fujiwara called one "naturalistic" and the other "nonrealistic." The naturalistic arrangements are those made of plant material that is seasonal and is arranged to represent its relative position in nature. The nonrealistic is an arrangement made with no regard to its habitat or growth. The modern abstract designs made in the Ohara school are usually labeled "nonrealistic."

Mrs. Fujiwara was a good teacher and each day she brought interesting plant material as we worked out the basic patterns together. For a first lesson she brought lotus leaves and buds. This was a lesson in the upright style. When I admired the lotus, Mrs. Fujiwara said "The lotus is a symbol of encouragement to man. It represents the aspirations of man with a promise of fulfillment. It has its origin in mud, but grows tall and strong and beautiful as it reaches toward heaven."

A heavy needle-point holder in an oval-shaped white dish called a *suiban* was a receptacle for the lotus upright arrangement. (Fig. 38.) The first stem placed in the holder a little to the front Mrs. Fujiwara called *shu-shi*. Another name for this branch, she said, was "subject." This was a tall, large lotus leaf. The second stem to be placed was a smaller leaf that was just unfolding. She called this one *fuku-shi* or secondary, and cut it two thirds the length of the first stem. This stem was placed to the left and front of the *shu-shi*. *Kyaku-shi* is the name given to the third stem, which is also called "object." This stem is cut very short and faces the viewer. Mrs. Fujiwara used a lotus leaf that almost seemed to float on the water for the *kyaku-shi*. The other stems are called *chukan*, or fillers, and are placed as supports to the main stem. I was surprised that the beautiful buds were not used as main lines, but in this arrangement they are secondary in importance. One tall bud was placed in back of the *shu-shi*, slanting a little backwards. Another bud, cut shorter, was placed in back of the *kyaku-shi*, and the third filler was a leaf that was just opening. It was placed behind the very short *kyaku-shi*. I was told that the fillers may be placed wherever they will do the most for the arrangement. Mrs. Fujiwara taught me the trick of placing one pin holder on top of the edge of another to keep a heavy arrangement from tipping. (Fig. 41a.)

Her second lesson was in the contrasting style using clipped palm and chrysanthemums. The *shu-shi*, a strong straight stem of

Figure 38 *For my first lesson my teacher brought lotus leaves and buds for an Ohara upright style:* (1) *subject,* (2) *secondary,* (3) *object.*

Figure 39 *Ohara contrasting style. This style of Japanese* ikebana *could easily be adapted for Western use:* (1) *subject,* (2) *secondary,* (3) *object.*

clipped palm, was measured twice the width of the flat oval dish. The *kenzan* was placed to the front left of the dish and the second stem, also of clipped palm, was placed close to the main stem in the holder and cut half the length. The contrasting style looks very much like the beginning of our crescent design. The *kyaku-shi,* or object stem is cut a third of the length of the *fuku-shi,* or secondary stem. The yellow chrysanthemums were used for this part of the arrangement. As soon as the main branches are placed, additional clipped palm and yellow chrysanthemums may be placed according to the taste of the arranger. This style of Japanese *ikebana* could easily be adapted for Western use. (Fig. 39.)

I interpreted the Ohara heavenly style when I returned home in the spring with rhubarb blossoms and foliage from my vegetable garden. I used a deep yellow-green pottery vase with slanting sides and a *kenzan* (needle-point holder) secured in the bottom of the container.

The subject (Heaven) branch is measured by the width "plus" depth of the container. The secondary (Man) branch cut half the length of the subject, is placed in front of it and the object (Earth) is cut one third of the secondary branch and placed facing the viewer. Rhubarb blossoms seem to have an ethereal quality suitable for heavenly style. The foliage is deeply veined and textured with a quality and bold form suitable for modern design. (Fig. 40.)

One of the most popular styles in the Ohara method is the *moribana* slanting style. (Fig. 41a–d.) This is a relatively simple basic design. The *kenzan* is placed in any one of the four corners of the dish. The corner is determined in a round dish by drawing an imaginary square in the dish. The subject stem is placed to left or right front of dish extending out from it at a sharp angle. The secondary stem is cut two thirds the length of the subject and is placed at about a fifty-degree angle to the left. The object is cut to one half the length of the secondary and placed at an angle facing the viewer.

A variation of the slanting style is called "water viewing." (Plate 12.) The subject or Heaven branch extends over the expanse of water in the dish with the *kenzan* in left or right front or back of the dish. The other stems are measured in the same way they are for the basic slanting style, i.e., subject, one and a half times the width and depth of dish; secondary, two thirds of subject; object, one half of secondary.

In Kyoto I lived in a charming Japanese inn where the proprietress had been a student of the Ohara school. Each day a lovely Ohara arrangement was placed in the *tokonoma* in my room. All the basic designs, i.e., upright, slanting, heavenly, cas-

Figure 40 Ohara heavenly style. Rhubarb blossoms and
leaves have an ethereal quality suitable for this design:
(1) subject, (2) secondary, (3) object.

Figure 41a-d *The Japanese chrysanthemum, "Mrs. Osaka," is arranged in one of the most popular styles in the Ohara method, called the* moribana *slanting style. This is a relatively simple basic design:* (1) *subject,* (2) *secondary,* (3) *object.*

cading, and contrasting, may be arranged in either the *moribana* or *heikwa* style. The technique for making the branches secure in the *heikwa* style in the Ohara method is very much like those used in the Ikenobo way. (Fig. 27.)

The Ohara cascade style might also be called *nageire*. It is very much like the *nageire* style in the other schools of Japanese *ikebana*. The Heaven or subject branch, is the longest branch. It cascades out of the tall receptacle with the Man, or secondary branch placed next, also partially swinging out. The Earth, or object, may be represented by blossoms or other stems or branches. A cascade arrangement made with branches of flowering magnolia and one of pine branches and red anemones illustrates this style. The container is white pottery made in a traditional *heikwa* design. (Fig. 42a and b.) Almost any tall, slim vase is suitable

for a *nageire* arrangement. Although the translation of *nageire* in English means "throw in," I learned that the *nageire ikebana* is arranged with great care.

There is a legend about how the name *nageire* came about. It was customary for the noble samurai in the ancient days of Japan to take their tea masters with them when they went to battle. After a long, hard day, when the Tea Ceremony was about to be performed, the tea master found he had no means of holding the flowers in place for the *ikebana* part of the ritual. He took his sword, tied it to the flowers and threw it into the water of the container. The flowers fell in such an artistic, pleasing design, that the noble warrior said how much he liked this "throw-in" style of arrangement. From then on the *nageire* style was imitated and became one of the popular patterns for arranging flowers in all the schools of Japanese *ikebana*.

The heavenly style is a stately vertical pattern. The heavenly Ohara arrangement in Fig. 43 was made with plant material native

Figure 42a *Magnolia blossoms are arranged in a spring arrangement in the cascade* heikwanageire *style.*

Figure 42b *In the same vase an Ohara cascade* heikwa *style is made with pine and anemones:* (1) *subject,* (2) *secondary,* (3) *object.*

to Hawaii in an unusual glass container. Ti leaves, gladioli buds, and pale pink anthurium blossoms are arranged in this simple style. The *moribana* heavenly style in Plate 13 allowed for freedom of design once the main stems were placed. The plant material is unusual. Rhubarb chard with its dark foliage and red stem and veins seemed quite appropriate with bright red zinnias in a dark copper dish, to illustrate this design in the Ohara way.

Figure 43 *Ti leaves and pink anthurium from Hawaii provide simple but interesting material for a heavenly* heikwa *arrangement in a modern green glass bottle.* (1) *subject,* (2) *secondary,* (3) *object.*

Figure 44   *A few Easter lilies, coleus foliage, and one branch of man-*
zanita create a lovely Ohara water-viewing design: (1) *subject,* (2)
secondary, (3) *object.*

Glass is not often used for traditional Japanese flower arrangements, but the modern masters sometimes take liberties in the
selection of containers for *ikebana.* The arrangement in the long-
necked bottle is such an exception. Grape ivy, camellia buds, foliage, and blossom are composed in a *nageire* cascading-style arrangement inspired by the Ohara master, Mr. Houn Ohara. (Plate
14.)

Of all the four schools in which I studied, I considered the
Ohara school the most like our Western way with flowers and
the easiest to understand and execute. The designs are simple and
the holder is the needle-point kind that we use in the United
States. (Fig. 44.)

CHAPTER VIII

Sogetsu School

One of the talents of the Japanese artist is "to embody beauty in a form of imperfection or even ugliness." How true this observation seemed when I tried to understand and appreciate the original designs of the modern flower master, Mr. Sofu Teshigahara of the. Sogetsu school in Tokyo.

I studied in the Sogetsu school when I was in Japan and I found it a very interesting and stimulating experience. I had heard a good deal about it in the United States before leaving for Japan. Many conservative *ikebana* students had warned me of the extreme and unusual character of this modern expression of the flower art of Japan. I went with an open mind, however, and I am so glad I studied in this wonderful new school.

The history of the Sogetsu school is really the life history of its founder, Mr. Sofu Teshigahara. In the late 1800s Mr. Sofu's father, Hisatsuga Teshigahara, was a teacher in one of the popular ancient classical schools of the time. His son, Sofu, followed in his father's footsteps and at the early age of fifteen was already a *sensei*, assisting his father. In 1926 he had a flower show exhibition of his free-style designs made with plants and flowers. The popularity of his modern ideas grew rapidly. Of course, there were many who severely criticized the teacher when he was young. Japan is a country steeped in tradition. The use of *ikebana* for modern artistic expression was a new idea, but it had special appeal to the young people of Japan. The Pacific war interrupted further progress of the Sogetsu school. As soon as the war was over there was a tremendous rebirth of interest in *ikebana* and a particular interest in modern styles in music, painting, drama, and dress. Modern free-style *ikebana* felt the trend and had a ready acceptance at this time.

When I arrived in Tokyo, the Sogetsu Art Center, a beautiful new modern building, had just been completed. It was my pleasure to attend the formal opening of this significant monument to modern *ikebana* at the October meeting of the Ikebana International Society. Mr. Sofu gave a dramatic demonstration of free-style designs in the striking red and gold auditorium. Murals in the style of Picasso decorated the walls. The audience was a distinguished gathering of Japanese and foreign dignitaries from all over the world. Nearly all foreign visitors and temporary residents of Japan are interested in *ikebana*. After the program a social tea was served on the terrace in the rear of the building. Modern sculpture is a permanent part of the decoration here, and as the bright spotlights fell on the modern *roji* and the interesting stone sculpture, the pretty little Japanese ladies in their exquisite kimonos and obis presented a picture of sharp contrasts. The ladies who assisted Mr. Sofu on stage wore beautiful Japanese kimonos also.

Mrs. Taguchi, one of these attractive ladies and a senior instructor at the Sogetsu school, was my teacher. She came to my quarters at the International House to give me private lessons. With special instruction and because of my experience with *ikebana* for many years in the United States, I progressed rapidly. I was taught to construct two and sometimes three flower arrangements for each lesson. My teacher drilled me thoroughly in the basic principles. She wished me to be prepared to attend the advanced class at the Sogetsu Art Center where Mr. Sofu, the master, taught free style. It interested me to learn that even in this extremely "modern" school the trinity of "Heaven, Man, and Earth" were present in all *ikebana*. The name for the Heaven branch is *shin*, the Man branch is *soe*, and the branch known as Earth is called *hikae* in the Sogetsu school.

I will always remember one of my first lessons as Mrs. Taguchi and I sat on our knees, Japanese fashion, one warm September afternoon, at the International House. "We will make an arrangement in the upright style," said my teacher. (Fig. 45a–c.) The *kenzan* is placed in either the left or right front of the shallow dish for this *moribana* style. *Shin* is measured by one and a half times the width and depth of the dish. It is placed at an angle of approximately forty-five degrees. (Fig. 45b.) The second stem, *soe*,

Figure 45a-c *To demonstrate the Sogetsu upright, variation 1, I arranged pussy willow and white ranunculus in a square black pottery dish:* (1) shin, (2) soe, (3) hikae.

is measured three fourths the length of *shin* and is placed at a seventy-five-degree angle. *Hikae* is three fourths the length of *soe* and is placed facing the viewer at about a fifteen-degree angle. (Fig. 45b.) The remaining stems are cut and arranged according to the personal taste of the designer. These stems are called *mai* (fillers or supports). To demonstrate this design variation I used white ranunculus in a square black pottery shallow container. (Fig. 45c.)

The slanting *moribana* style is also constructed in a variety of patterns. Again the *shin* branch is measured approximately one and a half times the width and depth of the dish, the *soe* is three fourths the length of the *shin*, and the *hikae* is three fourths the length of the *soe*. The angle and position in the *kenzan* differs with each variation. The Sogetsu slanting style variation VI is similar to one in the Ohara method called the water-viewing slanting style. I used torch ginger, manzanita, rubber leaves, and coleus foliage to illustrate this design. Torch ginger represents *shin*, the rubber leaf *soe*, and the coleus is *hikae* in my interpretation of this variation. (Fig. 46.)

The *nageire* is also very popular in the Sogetsu school. I enjoyed making a *nageire* slanting style in a basket I bought in Kyoto. I made the arrangement of bleached mulberry vine and red roses and displayed the arrangement on a wooden burl. The rose, placed at a forty-five-degree angle, represents *shin*; the bud, placed at a fifteen-degree angle is *soe*; and the short-stemmed rose is *hikae*, placed at approximately a seventy-five-degree angle. (Plate 15.) Branches of bamboo shrub with a dahlia in a celadon green vase is a free style variation of the *nageire* style.

The same proportions are used in placing flowers in the Sogetsu slanting style in both the *heikwa* or the *moribana* style. The various ways of securing the stems and branches for the *nageire* style do not vary much with the different schools. I found they all use the same tricks as were originated in the Ikenobo method. (Fig. 29.) (Plate 18.)

The advanced classes I attended in the Sogetsu Art Center were very interesting. Before they began the students were permitted to select a flower container from a large assortment of unusual ceramics designed especially for Mr. Sofu. Each student could select flowers in two varieties for the day's lesson, but there were

Plate 15   The Sogetsu slanting style, variation 2, is a
nageire arrangement that I made in a basket with mulberry
vine and roses: (1) shin, (2) soe, (3) hikae.

Plate 16   Tangled driftwood and anemones dramatize the
sharp contrast between the gnarled wood and perfect budding
anemone (Sogetsu free style): (1) shin, (2) soe, (3) hikae.

Plate 17   Southern pine and roses are happily combined in
a simple Enshu pattern: (1) shin, (2) gyo, (3) otoshi.

Plate 18   Nageire free
style (Sogetsu school)
illustrated by the
bamboo shrub (poly-
gonum paronychia) and
an apricot dahlia: (1)
shin, (2) soe, (3) hikae.

Plate 19   A traditional hanging
container of the classical school may be
employed for a simple design in
the modern Sogetsu method. A single
camellia with a few curving wisteria
vines provide the plant material for an
interesting design: (1) shin, (2) soe,
(3) tai.

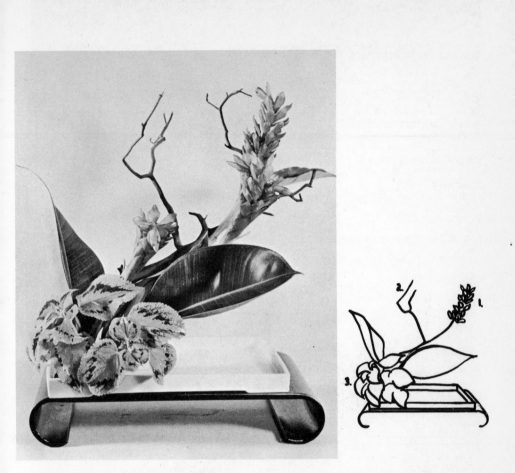

Figure 46 *The Sogetsu slanting style, variation 6, lends itself to a combination of torch ginger, a rubber leaf, coleus foliage, and driftwood:* (1) shin, (2) soe, (3) hikae.

no restrictions on the design, vase or flowers. It was free style and a kind of "free for all" before getting started. Each student had a table to work on. Mr. Sofu went from student to student making suggestions and commenting on the great variety of ideas expressed there. Most of the advanced students are interested in creating abstract designs. Sometimes it is not plant material. Combinations of wood, stone and metal are used. Intricate designs are created by pyramiding branches of driftwood that have curves and bends. A few lovely blossoms may be added to the picture. Manzanita and driftwood branches with anemone create a dramatic effect (Plate 16) in the Sogetsu way. Large clawlike branches

Figure 47 A maze of cherry blossoms and anemones illustrates the
Japanese way of half-concealing a lovely blossom. The Sogetsu free
style allows for imaginative arrangements: (1) shin, (2) soe, (3) hika

Figure 48 *The Florida shore inspired an arrangement of clipped palm and sea grape leaves silhouetted against a* shoji *screen (Ikenobo school):* (1) shin, (2) soe, (3) tai.

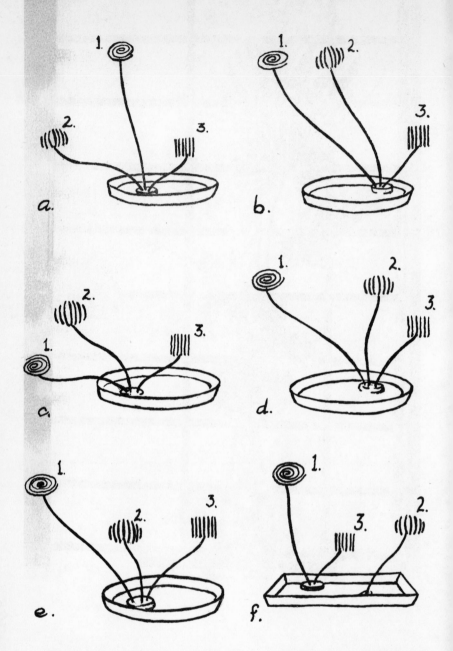

Figure 49a *The six basic designs most generally used in the Sogetsu school in the* moribana *style are:* (a) *upright,* (b) *slanting style, principle I,* (c) *horizontal,* (d) *slanting style, variation 1,* (e) *slanting style, variation 2,* (f) *upright style, variation 5.*

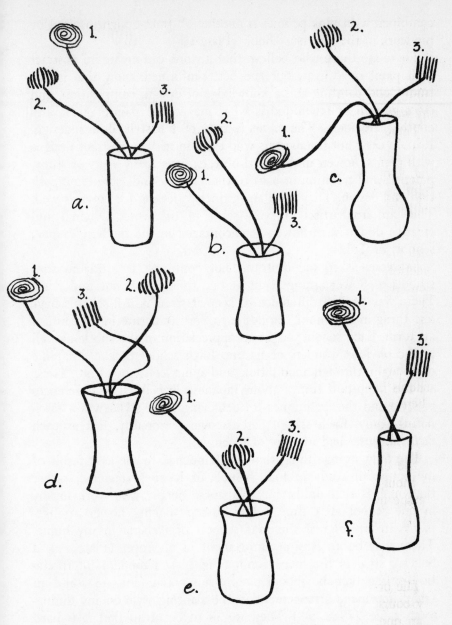

Figure 49b *The six basic designs most generally used in the Sogetsu school for the* heikwa *style are:* (a) nageire *upright,* (b) nageire *slanting style,* (c) nageire *hanging style,* (d) nageire *slanting style, variation 1,* (e) *slanting style, variation 2,* (f) nageire *upright style, variation 4.*

combined with pink peonies is another abstract design inspired by my work in the Sogetsu school. (Plate 20.)

There are those who believe that anyone can create an abstract with paint on canvas, but the better-informed know this is not true. Good painting and a knowledge of design, composition, and color as well as technique is what makes one painter great and another mediocre. The same is true of free-style flower design. It looks easy, but the masters who excel in making abstract designs with plants, flowers and related objects, have many years of study, practice, and tradition in back of them. They understand composition and design. They have an instinctive feeling for color as well. They are true artists in every sense of the word. Original and creative design with flowers is encouraged in the modern *ikebana* schools of Tokyo.

Everyone asked me if it was not confusing to study in four schools of flower arrangement at one time. I did not find it so. There was enough difference to keep it straight. All schools have one thing in common: the desire to portray nature in a beautiful art form. Each school taught an appreciation of the subtle as well as the obvious wonders of nature. Each school taught discipline of thought through meditation and quiet contemplation. These are the important things about Japanese *ikebana*. The differences of style and the techniques for achieving these styles was a fascinating study. Each school had its own personality, just as each *ikebana sensei* had his way of teaching.

The only strange thing that has happened to me as a result of my course of study in four schools of Japanese *ikebana*, rather than one, is that unlike most Japanese people who work loyally in one school at a time I find myself making flower arrangements in any one of the four schools of *ikebana* in my home. There may be an Enshu arrangement in my foyer (Plate 17), a Sogetsu style in the living room (Fig. 47), a modern interpretation of the Ikenobo school on my sun porch (Fig. 48), and an Ohara *moribana* arrangement in the slanting style on my dining-room table. (Plate 21.) They are all so beautiful that it is hard to know which I prefer. I feel a little like the pianist who enjoys playing the musical compositions of many fine composers. (Fig. 49a and b.)

"He who views the perfect beauty of a rose becomes filled with its reflected beauty."

CHAPTER IX

Japanese Receptacles

The receptacle in which a Japanese flower arrangement is made is of great importance. The choice of this vessel could hardly be called haphazard. Its selection does not depend on good taste alone or the relationship of container and flowers in form, color and texture, as it usually is in the West.

Many centuries of tradition have dictated not only the designs of Japanese flower arrangements, but also the style of receptacle best suited for each kind of flower and the occasion for which it is arranged. This is particularly true when flowers are arranged in the classical way like that of the Ikenobo or Enshu schools. The modern schools (i.e., Ohara and Sogetsu) allow for more freedom in the selection in the style of container. In some modern free-style *ikebana* the receptacle is more important than the flowers. (Plate 17.)

The first receptacles for flowers were brought to Japan from China by Buddhist priests. They were urn-shaped, made of bronze and intended for early *rikkwa* styles of *ikebana* displayed in the temples and shrines. Later, as *ikebana* became a part of the Tea Ceremony, the design of the flower containers became modified. A tall, cylindrical bronze vase, sometimes with a trumpet-shaped opening, was designed for this purpose. It is not uncommon to find this early style of vase supported by a dragon, a turtle, a frog, a serpent, or even what appears to be waves from the sea or clouds. The Japanese name for this style of receptacle is *kwa-bin*. No matter what the material a Japanese flower container is made of, the basic reasons for its selection are its appropriateness for the occasion, its suitability to the plant material to be arranged in it, and its enhancement of the beauty of nature.

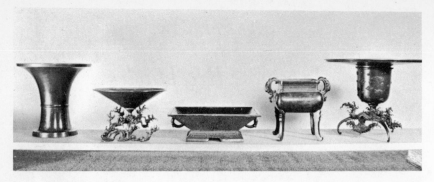

Figure 50 *Bronze containers are popular for Japanese classical and* modern ikebana.

Figure 51 A *bronze* usubata *designed especially for the Enshu school* arranged in the fall with pussy willows and dahlias: (1) shin, (2) gyo, (3) otoshi.

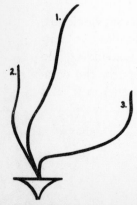

BRONZE

There is good reason why one of the most popular vessels used for flowers in Japan is made of bronze. Bronze is the color of the earth. It may be cast in many beautiful designs and it is almost indestructible. Flower containers made of this enduring metal are the kind most admired by Western flower arrangers. (Fig. 50.) I was fortunate to find the cone-shaped *usubata* used in Figure 51 many years ago in an antique shop in Connecticut. The larger one with a removable disc is an antique that my teacher helped select when I was in Tokyo. Both of these containers are right for the Enshu style. (Fig. 30.) The very simple classical bronze vase with no decoration used in Figure 52 is typical of the kind suggested for the Ikenobo method.

Figure 52 *The bronze container characteristic of the Ikenobo school is simple and sturdy of design. It is well-related to the beautiful Japanese umbrella pine and anemones. Attractive tables and stands are used under Japanese classical* ikebana: (1) shin, (2) soe, (3) tai.

Figure 53 A *bronze* sunabachi *is a traditional shallow container for
an Ikenobo* moribana *arrangement of iris:* (1) shin, (2) soe, (3) tai.

There are shallow-dish type containers made of bronze, called
sunabachi. (Fig. 53.) They were originally intended for small land-
scapes and the name translated means "sand bowl." Informal
rikkwa arrangements were often made in this type of receptacle.
It was this shallow-dish design in which Mr. Houn Ohara's grandfather, Unshin Ohara, probably made the first *moribana*-style
flower arrangement. Shallow dishes are extremely popular in all the
schools. They are considered particularly suitable for arrangements of water plants and flowers. It is easy to create a naturalistic
effect of a water scene in this type of container. (Plate 22.)

Bronze is generally associated with a formal style of *ikebana.*
It symbolizes great endurance and an agelessness that is greatly

admired by the Japanese. Antique Chinese bronze vases are still found in Japan in the museums, and are highly prized as treasures by those people who own them. (Plate 17.)

It is not unusual to see bronze crescent-shaped receptacles (*tsuki-gata* or *gekko-gata*) hanging by chains from the molding above a window, door opening or in the *tokonoma* in Japanese homes. It is no wonder they are so popular. The arrangement of a vine and a single blossom in a hanging crescent with the sky as a background has an ethereal beauty. (Plate 19.)

POTTERY

The potters of Japan are famous. With the *Cha-no-yu* as an inspiration, great pride has been taken for at least five centuries in producing ceramic tea caddies, tea cups and *ikebana* receptacles that are worthy of this meaningful ceremony. One of the most beautiful shapes made of pottery is the tall, twelve-inch vase designed in many variations of the cylinder. There are some that are smaller at the base, gradually curving into a slight bulbous effect at the neck. (Fig. 54.) This style has become traditionally associated with the *nageire* style of *ikebana*. There are other pottery vases made in slim, elliptical forms very much like our Western styles. There are round, shallow bowls and oblong dishes called

Figure 54 *Pottery vases for* heikwa *arrangements are simple in design. They are used in all the* ikebana *schools, classical and modern.*

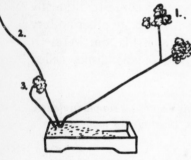

Figure 55 *Pink flowering Bechtel crab apple arranged in a celadon-green pottery suiban in the Ohara slanting style:* (1) *subject,* (2) *secondary,* (3) *object.*

suiban. (Fig. 55.) Oval-shaped shallow bowls are designed in many sizes and variations, and like the simple, tall vase, are popular receptacles in use in all the flower-arrangement schools.

Until recently, glass has never been a very popular receptacle for flowers in Japan. Today modern flower masters find glass receptacles as inspiring as the pottery, wood, iron, stone, bamboo, gourds, and bronze. (Fig. 43 and Plate 14.) Flower receptacles used for modern free-style designs are not traditionally bound to any special kind of material. Imaginative abstract designs are made of metals and potteries, as well as the natural forms found in gnarled tree roots, driftwood, and bamboo. (Fig. 56.)

Figure 56 *Abstract ceramic art by Estelle Halper inspires an arrangement of star magnolia in the Sogetsu manner.*

BAMBOO

An extremely popular material from which flower containers are made in Japan is bamboo. It is so appropriate as a flower vessel, practically all the flower arrangement schools recommend its use. In Japan, bamboo is very common and inexpensive. It grows there in abundance. This does not take away from its distinctive possibilities as a natural flower container. So much ingenuity has been used through the centuries in creating unusual

Figure 57 *One of the simplest but loveliest bamboo containers is the plain cylinder about twelve inches high. An arrangement of zinnias, andromeda Japonica (Ikenobo school): (1) shin, (2) soe, (3) tai.*

and interesting containers from this material that even though many people own bamboo flower containers, there are no two exactly alike. (Fig. 57.)

There is a legend about the first time bamboo was used as a flower receptacle. In about the fifteenth century the great samurai, Toyotomi Hideyoshi was laying siege to Odawara Castle. The resistance to the siege was very stubborn. To keep his generals happy and relaxed, Hideyoshi had his tea master, Rikyu, perform the

Cha-no-yu. The proper utensils were not always available, so the legend goes. Rikyu conceived the idea of cutting a cylinder of bamboo to serve as a container for the *ikebana* that was such a beautiful part of the ceremony. He went to a neighboring bamboo grove where he found just the right-sized stalk. He cut the vase himself. As the bamboo dried it showed a crack. This mark became the characteristic mark of the vase. It has been known ever since as the "Onjoji vase." The Onjoji is a historical Buddhist temple near Lake Biwa. This temple has a bell in it with a crack (like our Liberty Bell). Because of this coincidence the cracked bamboo vase received the name of the temple. The crack gave Rikyu's vase a *sabi* quality greatly admired. The tea men of Japan consider this vase a sacred treasure because of its artistic merit and historical significance.

When green, bamboo is easily cut. The joints have natural complete separations so that the bamboo stalks can be cut apart to make containers which hold water. The better ones are manufactured today with a metal liner that prevents the possibility of leakage. When bamboo is shipped to the United States, the dry heat causes it to split unless it is well seasoned before it leaves Japan. This has discouraged the importation of these attractive receptacles for Western use. I found a way of preserving the bamboo containers that I shipped from Japan for my personal use by storing them in the cool, moist atmosphere of an unheated basement.

Great ingenuity has been used in the design of some of these containers. The simplest one, however, is the plain cylinder about twelve inches high. There is a two-story kind called a *niju-ike*. This type has a window cut in the lower section which allows for a very lovely double flower arrangement. The top section usually is arranged with tree branches that cascade out of it, and the lower section is frequently used for an arrangement of flowers. (Fig. 58.) There are many variations, some with three and four openings. One book illustrates twenty-eight different bamboo designs, another has illustrations of sixty-one possible variations.

My Ikenobo teacher was the first to introduce me to the use of bamboo flower containers. I thought at first that these containers were only recommended for this one old classical school. I learned, however, that my other teachers found bamboo flower receptacles

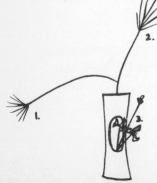

Figure 58 *The niju-ike is a two-story bamboo container that allows for very interesting Japanese ikebana. Umbrella pine represents the shin and soe and iris blossoms are the tai group for a niju arrangement (Ikenobo school).*

Figure 59a-e *Receptacles that are of a natural origin like a gourd, root, natural wood forms, fungus, bamboo, or stone have special appeal to the flower arranger in Japan. A piece of weathered wood in the natural form of a boat is an inspiring container for simple spring-flower arrangements. It is important in making an arrangement in the Ikenobo way to keep the collar on the base of the narcissus that holds the stem and foliage together naturally. When this is not possible, a piece of florist's plastic tape helps to create the same effect:* (1) shin, (2) soe, (3) tai.

just as acceptable for their method. By simply changing the type of *kubari* made to fit into the top and lower section, the container can be adapted for different techniques.

One of the most ingenious designs made out of bamboo is a hanging boat. (Fig. 25a and b.) The bow of the boat is cut at an angle that makes it look like a punt. The stern is cut bluntly. An oval opening is made for the cockpit in which a metal liner is fastened to hold water. Three chains are attached to the boat and brought together with a single hook so that the boat may be

Figure 60 A tall, narrow Japanese basket is a perfect container for the nageire style of flower arrangement. Weigela and peonies are easy garden flowers to practice with.

Figure 61 *There are beautiful modern as well as traditional baskets woven by experts in Japan.*

hung in a balanced position. This hook is sometimes fashioned in the shape of a monkey with one arm extended overhead and the other at its side to hold the chains.

GOURDS AND OTHER NATURALISTIC VASES FOR FLOWERS

Receptacles that are of natural origin, like gourds, roots, natural wood forms, fungi, bamboo, or stones, have special appeal to the flower arranger in Japan. The intention is to duplicate and glorify nature and this kind of container helps complete the naturalistic picture. (Fig. 59a–e.)

BASKETS

During the reign of Yoshimasa, the first woven baskets (*kago*) were employed for flowers. The designs were of Chinese origin and the basket weaver who introduced them to the great Shogun was a Chinese by the name of Hakoji. Yoshimasa was so pleased with the baskets woven by Hakoji he ordered many to be made by this fine weaver. Hakoji had a daughter named Reshojo who lived with him in his mountain hut. She was a fine weaver also. The baskets made by Hakoji were designed with a large handle. The ones his daughter made had no handle. For this reason these baskets became known as *Hakoji Gata Kago* and *Reshojo Gata Kago* to describe these two original basket designs. (Fig. 60.)

I found some very beautiful old and new baskets when I was in Tokyo. They seemed particularly well suited to flowers arranged in an informal style. Each basket is fitted with a bamboo cylinder that holds water. (Fig. 61.)

FLOWER RECEPTACLES FOR WALL BRACKETS (KAKE BANAIKE)

Many Japanese flower containers are made with a special hook so that they may be used hung on the wall. Baskets, bamboo, gourds, and containers made of pottery and bronze are suitable for this purpose. They are usually miniature in size. The simple, informal type of arrangement is often used very subtly in the home, on a small wall space near the entrance door, in the bathroom, or on a small wooden panel in the *tokonoma*. Gourds are very adaptable for this purpose.

Our concern so far has been with the material of which Japanese flower containers are made and their design. The artist who makes these receptacles usually has in mind the kind of flowers that will enhance the beauty of the entire composition. The color of most Japanese containers are neutral—black, white, green, gray, and brown are hues that blend with the color of the earth and its natural surroundings. There is no danger that these colors will compete with the flowers. Receptacles for flowers arranged in the Japanese way are not usually decorated with colorful design. Sometimes designs are embossed or attached to a Japanese flower container as a significant symbolism.

Old flower-arrangement manuscripts even dictate the appropriate flowers to be used in bronze, bamboo, pottery, and woven baskets. Some list the kind of flower vessels considered proper to use at different seasons of the year and others list the kind of flowers and how they should be arranged for special occasions. The size of the arrangement, the position of the branches and the color of the flowers have special symbolic meaning. Some of these ancient rules are still adhered to, but today there is generally a relaxation in the rigidity of the old dictates. (Fig. 62.) Even the classical schools have adopted freedom of choice in selection of

Figure 62 *Even the Ikenobo classical school keeps abreast of the times. A modern interpretation of Mt. Fuji with iris buds and cloud effects arranged by my Ikenobo teacher, Mrs. Usuda, in Tokyo.*

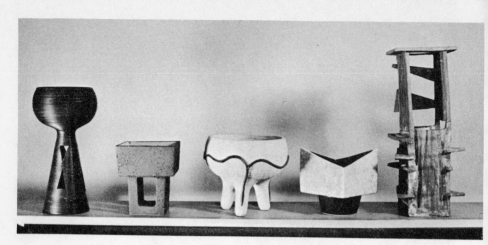

Figure 63 *It is possible to find interesting containers of modern design appropriate for* ikebana.

plant material and vase, although they make recommendations to the beginning student. (Fig. 63 and Fig. 64.)

It helps to appreciate and view *ikebana* more intelligently as it is displayed in Japan if you understand the thought and intention placed in an arrangement of flowers.

FORMAL, INTERMEDIATE, AND INFORMAL STYLE

The Japanese classify all of their arts in three possible moods: the formal, the intermediate, and the informal. Flower containers, plants, and flowers are classified as appropriate for use in these three styles. The flower-arrangement design is considered to be in one of these three categories according to the degree of rigidity, curve, or looseness given the general outline of the arrangement. Oversimplification is unwise, but it may help the beginner in the study of Japanese flower arrangement to know that (1) the urn-shaped bronze vessels identified with early *rikkwa* are most often used for formal arrangements (sometimes a simple bamboo cylinder (*sungiri*) is termed suitable for this formal style also); (2) containers with a wide mouth made of bronze, generally known as *usubata*, are recommended for intermediate arrangements; (3) shallow dishes, hanging receptacles, wall brackets, gourds, and tiered bamboo containers are considered informal in nature.

Figure 64 A *bisque pottery container arranged in a So-getsu free-style mood of bare branches and hydrangea blossoms.*

SEASONS AND VASES

In the spring the intermediate type of container is preferable. There should not be too much water showing. Bronze and bamboo are very appropriate for spring branches and flowers. In the summer, shallow-dish type vessels are practical. These arrangements are considered informal. A large expanse of water in the dish has a cooling, soothing effect on the viewer. Hanging containers are used at this time of year also. Baskets are permissible from spring to autumn, but not in winter. For winter the narrow-mouth type of receptacle is suggested made of bronze, pottery, or bamboo. Gourds are also used at this season. The pumpkin gourd is particularly admired for winter arrangements when snow is on the ground. It is often designed with a window cut through so the flowers may be seen from both sides.

The famous Sendensho (1450–1550) listed flowers under the following classifications:

1. Coming of age ceremony (*genbuku*).
2. Becoming a priest.
3. Common people entertain their superiors.
4. Going to war.
5. Moving house.
6. For prayer.
7. For use in the *tokonoma*.
8. For arrangement in corner of reception room.
9. For hanging flower vase.
10. Bridge from one room to the other (hanging).
11. Flowers for corridor.
12. Flowers for Tanabata Festival (seventh day of the seventh month).
13. Flowers for use in Buddhist temple.
14. Flowers for auspicious occasions.
15. Flowers for wedding.
16. Flowers to welcome guest.
17. Flowers for condolence.

Part Three
JAPANESE GARDENS

日本の庭園

When the land is bare
And the fields are colourless
There is most to see.
Better than the autumn tints
Is this lack of colour scheme.

Kare-hatete
Naka-naka tsuyu no
Aki yori mo.
Iro naki nōbe no
Iro nomi ni shimu.

Figure 65 *The distant, intermediate, and close views are illustrated in a Japanese garden as they are in a Japanese flower arrangement.*

CHAPTER X

Elements of a Japanese Garden

When I went to Japan I learned that there is a strong link between all the arts and cultures. I could not study one without being conscious of its relationship to the other. This is particularly true of Japanese gardens and Japanese *ikebana*. If *ikebana* is the Japanese way of keeping a reminder of the beauty of nature in the home, the Japanese garden goes a step further. Here nature is symbolized in a broader sense. It represents the universe and is intended to make man conscious of his relationship to it.

Without study it may be difficult for the average Occidental viewing a Japanese garden for the first time to understand the many subtleties in its design. If you are the kind of a person who associates the word "garden" with an abundance of colorful flowers, you may be a little surprised and disappointed to find that the gardens of Japan contain few flowers and very little color. Rocks, trees, shrubs, pebbles, gravel, sand, and water are the instruments by which the garden designer tells his story. Just as *ikebana* contains the three symbols of Heaven, Man, and Earth in a related pattern to each other, the design of a Japanese garden is made to illustrate the relationship of man to his deity in a broader sense.

The elements used in a Japanese garden are called Earth, Water, Fire, Wind, and Ether. In the ancient *rikkwa* flower arrangement you may remember, a natural scene was symbolized by using large, tree-like branches for the distant view. Shrubs and smaller trees were for the intermediate view and flowers for the close view. This is also true in the design of a Japanese garden. There is usually a formula and the garden designer respects this as he places the stone, sand, trees, and shrubs to illustrate his philosophy.

The largest stone is called the "guardian stone" and sometimes represents a mountain in the landscape. Smaller stones are placed around it like small hills and valleys in a natural landscape. If there is no natural place for a waterfall, a stone and a tree close to it become an imaginary one. Small hills and valleys are made a part of the scene. The trees and shrubs are often used to indicate a distant view, an intermediate view, and a close view. (Fig. 65.) If there is no natural water present in the garden scene, the effect of water is given by using sand and gravel. The sand is raked in a pattern to look like ripples on the water surface. (Fig. 66.) Blue-gray gravel is substituted for water in the brook.

A Japanese landscape may have a guest island and a master's island, sometimes symbolized by stones with moss or grass planted around them. A "worshiping stone" is the name given a flat one placed in the foreground. Trees and shrubs frequently provide a background.

I was charmed to learn that objects are often intentionally half-concealed in a Japanese garden. Everything must not be too apparent, they say. There must be something more than you see at a glance. It is purposely arranged so that a visitor to the garden may discover for himself some lovely little plant or ornament that is partially hidden from view. Mr. Jiro Hirada explains it beautifully in his book, A Glimpse of Japanese Ideals, when he says: "People take keen delight in concealing something charming in their gardens which can be discerned only by a keen observer, just as they enjoy doing kind deeds to others in secret to be found out, if at all, only by accident." (Fig. 47 and 67.)

The art of garden making was brought to Japan from China as early as the third century A.D. Picturesque little gardens, composed mainly of a pond or lake with an island in the center connected by small bridges, were a luxury that only the nobility could afford. Records tell of noblemen who owned gardens containing pines, willow, cherry, plum, and peach trees, and even chrysanthemums, orchids, carnations, and wisteria bloomed there. At this time the garden was simply a pretty place to enjoy for its design and color. It was also used for recreation. It was a great luxury that only the wealthy landowner could afford, like a fine painting or rare gem.

The change-over from the typical Chinese-style garden to what is generally recognized as a Japanese garden was a slow process. The abolition of the feudal system made land available for small private homes and gardens. Each era contributed changes in the way of applying the Buddhist philosophy to Japanese everyday living. Superstitions, as well as religious doctrines, were woven into the pattern. From the beginning there were many interpretations of the Tea Ceremony. Each tea master has his own way of designing the garden adjacent to the *chaseki* (teahouse). The important thing to observe is that the Japanese garden developed a shrine-like quality very much like the *tokonoma* in the house.

It was during the reign of Yoshimasa (1436–1490), the great Shogun of the Ashakaga Dynasty, that all of the arts of Japan

Figure 66 *Sand is raked to look like ripples on the water in the famous rock garden of Ryoan-ji Temple, Kyoto, Japan.*

Figure 67   *"People take keen delight in concealing something charming in their gardens which can be discerned only by a keen observer."*

came into flower. Yoshimasa was a great patron of the arts and all the artists of the day were encouraged to make their contribution to beautifying the Buddhist ceremonials. As we read in a former chapter, it was Saomi who formulated the artistic designs to improve the floral offerings in the temples and in the *tokonoma*. He was also responsible for designing some of the beautiful gardens connected with the temples and teahouses. Saomi is credited with having planned the garden surrounding the Kinkakuji (Golden Pavilion) in Kyoto which still stands. (Plate 1.) Kobori Enshu, the famous tea and flower master, was also responsible for some of the first gardens planned.

Cha-no-yu, the ancient Tea Ceremony of the Japanese people,

Figure 68 *Moss and lichens give a stone lantern a* sabi *quality. Note artistic straw coverings for plant protection.*

was developed during this period. One of its founders was the famous tea master of all time, Sen-No-Rikyu. With the development of the *Cha-no-yu* (Chap. III), *ikebana* and the garden became an important part of the significant religious and philosophical meaning of the whole ceremony. There were three styles of gardens, a formal style (*shin*), a less formal one (*gyo*), and a naturalistic style (*so*).

SABI AND WABI

There was a very special ingredient contained in the philosophy of Zen Buddhism that found expression in both the Japanese garden and Japanese *ikebana*. The Japanese words to describe this special quality are *sabi* and *wabi*. Both of these words have similar meaning applied to different things. According to my understanding, they are the descriptive words used to extol the beauty found in the simplest form of nature. The lichens and moss on a stone lantern give it a quality of mellowness that is often described as *sabi*. (Fig. 68.) *Sabi* describes the glorification of beauty found in the bare simplicity of the tearoom. *Sabi* is the ethereal quality we so admire in Japanese art. It is impossible to imitate a *sabi* quality unless there is complete sincerity. Anything that is artificial even though it creates the effect of simplicity and purity, lacks *sabi*.

Wabi, as I undersand it, describes the individual rather than the object. A life of *wabi* is often one of poverty where worldly etiquette is unimportant, for example, the life of a monk. The object of leading a life of *wabi* is to develop beauty from within. This, too, is the function of a Japanese garden. As we contemplate and meditate on its symbolic beauty, the mind and spirit are refreshed.

STONES

Stones are often used in Japanese gardens "to remind one by their shape and position, of some famous scene." Stones are so important to the garden designers of Japan that often men will spend months scouring the countryside for hundreds of miles just to locate one of special size, shape, color, and texture to fit into a garden landscape. There are legends told of the importance given the stones in a Japanese garden. One is about a rich merchant who commissioned a man to seek a special rock covered with moss and lichen as the "guardian stone" in his landscape. By the time the rock was finally located, three hundred miles away, and dragged out by oxen, so much time had elapsed and it had been so costly that the merchant went into bankruptcy. The beautiful moss-covered stone never reached its destination.

It is said that stones are particularly admired because they represent "solid reality, unchanging and enduring virtues, which are believed to have the power of softening the hardened hearts of men." Often the largest part of the stone is buried beneath the surface of the soil and only a small part is visible in the garden

Plate 20 Driftwood and peonies combine in a free-style arrangement in the Sogetsu way: (1) shin, (2) soe, (3) hikae.

Plate 21 The Ohara slanting style in a low dish of manzanita, zinnias, and coleus would provide a lovely summer arrangement for any Western dinner table: (1) subject, (2) secondary, (3) object.

Plate 22 An Ikenobo water-lily arrangement could be adapted for a Western dinner-table decoration: *(1)* shin, *(2)* soe, *(3)* tai.

Plate 23 An arrangement of grapes and foliage making an "S" curve on a glass plaque is a luncheon-table decoration both beautiful and economical.

Plate 24　An arrangement of geraniums and fantasy zinnias in an improvised wooden flower container that was formerly a part of an old newel post.

Plate 25 Crab apple blossoms and parrot tulips in an old
Chinese pottery shallow container would be at home in Tokyo
as well as New York.

scene. This is done to preserve the natural effect so that it looks as if it had always been there.

STEPPINGSTONES (TOBI-ISHI)

Steppingstones play a very important part in the design pattern of a Japanese garden. They give the garden a feeling of rhythm and motion. Sometimes they help to create the illusion of space or the mystery of beauty that lies just around the corner. Steppingstones may end with a shrub partly concealing the last stone. It appears to the viewer that the path continues. (Fig. 69.)

The steppingstones are usually slightly elevated above the soil in a Japanese garden. This is both a practical and an artistic technique. It is practical when, during the rainy season, the water does not drain off the soil quickly and the elevated stones serve a real purpose to keep from getting wet feet. The artistic application is to symbolize water by the use of gravel or sand, with the stepping-stones elevated as they would be if there were water surrounding them. (Fig. 70.) The selection of steppingstones for color, size, shape and texture is an art. A great deal of time is spent in finding these important garden accessories.

There are many kinds of trees and shrubs used in a Japanese landscape, but the most popular is the pine (*Pinus densiflora*) (*akanatsu*). Trees often form the background for a garden. Space for a garden is very limited and a background of trees creates the illusion of a natural setting. Also, trees act as a screen. A fence is generally incorporated with this natural background. In a country where land is at such a premium, a fence or wall acts as a shield from nearby buildings and gives the illusion of space. Privacy is essential also. Beautiful fences are designed of wood, bamboo, sticks, and grasses. Stone and cement are also used. (Fig. 71a–c.)

The mood and approach to designing a Japanese garden combines the spiritual desire to create an abode for a replica of nature with one that is fittingly beautiful. "A place for man to evaluate himself spiritually and see himself in the right proportion to the infinite," as Mr. Harada so aptly puts it.

Figure 69 *Steppingstones give the garden a feeling of rhythm and motion. They also provide the illusion of space.*

Figure 70 *Steppingstones are elevated for a practical as well as artistic effect. During the rainy season water does not drain off quickly and elevated steppingstones serve a real purpose.*

YO-IN

You may remember that every Japanese flower arrangement has its *yo* (sunny) side, and its *in* (shady) side. The same idea of *yo* and *in* is considered in designing and constructing a Japanese garden. The effect of light and shade in the garden is handled by the designer as an artist who places dark lines on a light canvas. *Yo* and *in* represents sharp contrasts in life as the Japanese person views his garden and sees the shadows and highlights. It represents the happy and sad, forces of good and evil, strong and weak, summer and winter, and any other of the many contrasts that we experience in living.

It is interesting to see the great variety of patterns that the Japanese garden designer finds possible with stone and trees, shrubs, sand and a few garden ornaments. Each object is placed in a pattern that relates a symbolic story to the viewer. As each movement of the *Cha-no-yu* is important to the ceremony, so is the placement of these garden elements significant and meaningful to the viewer.

Although in the West we appraise a garden by the lush growth of foliage and flowers as well as design, our taste is changing. It is not unusual to find modern homes with gardens and foundation plantings that are restrained in design. The plant material, used sparingly, is very much as it is in the gardens of Japan. Modern homes have doors and windows that slide away to reveal the beauty of a garden view. (Fig. 72.) The trend is to bring the outdoors and indoors together to extend living space.

Western home designers and landscape artists have found that the pleasing effect obtained by the use of sand, gravel, and stone has a popular appeal from an artistic and practical point of view. There have been periods when Western architects have poorly imitated Oriental gardens and in some places the meaningless examples still stand. Little pagodalike teahouses that were never used for tea, and stone lanterns and small bridges that cluttered up the landscape may still be seen.

To slavishly copy a Japanese garden without understanding seems as fruitless as making a Japanese flower arrangement without a sympathetic knowledge of the story it has to tell. With a little imagination a small Western home with limited space for a garden

Figure 71a–c *Japanese fences are an important part of the garden design. They are made of bamboo, wood, grasses and concrete.*

can become just as beautiful as the small gardens of Japan. In fact it may become a "real conversation piece" to the proud owner. How much more practical to put all the budget into the cost of one or two specimen trees or shrubs that may be trained into beautiful form and line than to spend it on space-filling shrubbery.

Figure 72 *Japanese homes have doors and windows that slide away to reveal the beauty of a garden view.*

Part Four
IDEAS EAST AND WEST

The red camellia can not tell
What secrets in the bosoms dwell
Of white camellia-trees that stand
Blowing serene so close at hand

Tonari naru shiroki tsubaki no fushigi woba
Toku sube shiranu benitsubaki kana
                    YOSANO AKIKO.

Figure 73 *There is a basic pattern even in mass arrange-ments. A Western-style Victorian arrangement of white snapdragons, tulips, freesias, and anemones with white and green caladium leaves, in a white alabaster compote.*

CHAPTER XI

Memo to My Japanese Friends: Western Flower Arrangement

The Japanese art of flower arrangement has had ever increasing popularity with Western people. As early as 1928 those who were interested in the relatively new art of arranging flowers were especially intrigued with the great beauty the Japanese were able to achieve with a few branches and flowers. Western-style flower arrangements had been made in the manner of the Dutch and Flemish painters. They were generally large masses of flowers and plant material grouped together in a bouquet of color with little thought to design. We still enjoy using masses of flowering material in the West. There are many who prefer these massive types of arrangements that apply the colors and forms of the flowers, like paint, to achieve an effect. A love for color and an extravagant way of using it may seem vulgar to those with more subtle tastes, but in some American and European homes masses of colorful flowers are better suited to the interior decoration.

It is not easy for those viewing an arrangement in the Japanese manner for the first time to recognize the difference between a Western-style line arrangement and authentic Japanese *ikebana*. The basic principles and elements of good design are often present in both. We are a very design-conscious nation with a growing appreciation for all forms of art. It is not surprising, then, that we have taken the artistic and charming Japanese way with flowers to our hearts even though our enthusiasm may seem a little exaggerated. To many who have never considered themselves artistic, flower arrangement has opened up a new world. Japanese flower arrangements look so simple and economical to execute that they have often been responsible for encouraging our Western flower designers to try their hand at it.

When I was in Japan, I was asked, "How is the art of flower arrangement different in the United States from the way we perform it here?" I tried to answer this question by saying, "In the West we use flower arrangement as an art form. We make arrangements of branches and flowers, observing the principles of *zuan* (design), i.e., *kincoo* (balance), *tsuriai* (proportion), *wariai* (scale), *sen* (line), *ritsudoo* (rhythm), *taisho* (contrast), *shihai* or *tsuyoi* (dominance), and *kurikaeshi* (repetition)."

We have learned from the Japanese way the three main lines of a flower arrangement you call 'Heaven, Man and Earth,' but we consider these the basic structural lines on which we build our flower design. All well-designed flower arrangements, according to to our Western standards, must have this basic structure. I would add, "Even if the flowers and foliages conceal this foundation (Fig. 73), it still must be there. The basic lines of a flower arrangement are like the armature made for a piece of sculpture modeled of clay. While most Japanese *ikebana* is triangular in design, our designs often take the form of a sphere, oval, rectangle, square, triangle, cone, spiral, rod, or strip." (Fig. 74.)

Another important element in a Western design made of plant material is color. We use color found already mixed in flowers, foliages, and branches, like paint. Colorful flowers are used in the West to augment the color scheme in interior home decoration. We use the "pigment theory" of combining and harmonizing color in the way we apply color in working with flowers and foliages. For example, we use a color spectrum to help us learn the application of the pigment theory to flower designs. We have learned how beautifully color hues termed *analogous*, closely related on the color spectrum, may blend. Tints and shades of yellow, green-yellow, green, and blue-green exemplify this harmony. Monochromatic harmonies or tints and shades of the same hue are often used in our flower designs. The plant materials of complementary and contrasting hues require more skill to combine artistically, and even more complicated are the color harmonies termed *triads* and *tetrads* of color.

Although in Japan flower arrangements contain a symbolic message, in the West our flower arrangements are most often intended as an artistic expression used mainly for decoration. Sometimes our flower arrangements are intended to express a message of

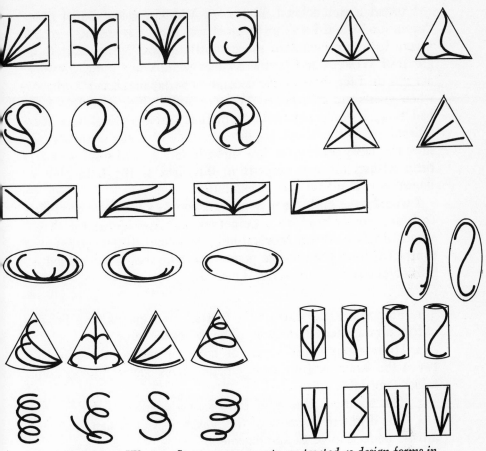

Figure 74 *Western flower arrangements are treated as design forms in great variety. The square, the sphere, the rectangle, oval, cone, spiral, cylinder, triangle, and strip illustrate these possibilities for design.*

condolence, affection, good luck, pleasant journey, or welcome home. The message is generally found on the card enclosed, rather than in the significant arrangement of the flowers.

The practice of combining seasonal branches and flowers is one we have adopted from Japanese *ikebana*. (Fig. 75.) There are some flower artists in both East and West who do not agree with this idea. They mix delicate tropical blossoms with the foliages of coarse vegetables and grasses, if the forms and colors create a pleasing effect.

I found a well-defined interest in Western-style "dinner-table decoration" when I was in Japan. I was sorry I could not accept a very flattering invitation to demonstrate this Western art to a group of Western and Japanese ladies while I was there. Flowers are not used for dinner-table decoration in Japan, except, perhaps, when guests are entertained Western style. (Fig. 76.) If I had had time, I would have told them that "table setting" is a specialized art in the West, requiring a study of many elements besides the table decoration. We often have a special display of artistic settings made by experts in this field at the time of our flower shows and for special exhibition.

I would have said, "It may interest you to know how carefully each accessory placed on a dinner table is considered for these special displays. When they are judged in competition, points are subtracted from the possible perfect score of 100, if the exhibitor fails to observe the following standards:

1. Proportion and scale of the plates, water glasses, and flower or fruit arrangement in relation to the size of the table.
2. Harmonious combination of color in the relationship between the flower or fruit arrangement, plates, glasses, flower container, and table cover.
3. The texture harmony of the accessories—plates, glasses, etc.
4. The distinctive quality of the flower or fruit design, and the artistic perfection of the arrangement.
5. The horticultural perfection of the flower or fruit used for the table decoration.

We observe the courteous custom of keeping the flower arrangement for a seated dinner low enough to see over when it is used in the center of a Western dinner table. We sometimes place the table decoration at the end of the table. The arrangement is designed taller for this occasion.

A buffet-style dinner is quite popular in the West. It enables the guests to help themselves and allows the hostess to serve many people at one time. The table decoration is generally tall for this kind of setting also.

The harmonious grouping of color is very important to suc-

Figure 75 *An arrangement of magnolia buds and tulips inspired by a Japanese seasonal arrangement.*

Figure 76 *Flowers are rarely placed on the Japanese luncheon table.*
A luncheon table set for two, Japanese style.

cessful table setting. Selecting harmonious flowers, plates, and table cover for an exhibition table setting helps win a first prize. Our contestants often determine their color scheme for a dinner table from the pattern (if there is one) in the dinner plate. If the dinner plate is plain, the inspiration may come from a harmonious group of flowers, fruits, or flowers and fruits combined.

I remember the lovely Japanese custom of being served with an individual tray, and the beautiful lacquer bowls and porcelain

Figure 77 *Western luncheon table. A crescent design of lilacs and peony-flowering tulips in shades of rose and mauve arranged in a copper shell set on a rose-colored damask table cover is a popular color combination.*

dishes that were a part of the service. I also recall nostalgically the relaxed, pleasant and unhurried atmosphere of the Japanese home in which I was a guest. How I wish I could have acquired the art of their serenity, along with the art of *ikebana*.

A design made in a crescent pattern (Fig. 77), similar to the Ohara contrasting style *moribana* (Fig. 39), would be very suitable for a Western dinner-table decoration. The slanting style of the Sogetsu method is an equally suitable design. (Fig. 46.) A floating arrangement of water lilies is a design associated with the Ikenobo method that makes a pleasing table centerpiece. (Plate 22.)

In the West, flower arrangements are used in the home to help the homemaker decorate the room interiors artistically. Flower arrangements are placed in strategic positions to purposely repeat the color in a chair covering or cushion or a painting. The flower designs are made to compliment the table or wall space they fill. Interior decorating or room design is an art that includes the Western art of flower arrangement.

We have found that Japanese *ikebana* suits our Western interior decoration very well in many instances. Strong, bold patterns are very harmonious with our contemporary homes that are often quite Eastern in feeling. (Fig. 32.) Even our period interiors that favor the seventeenth century are well adapted to the use of Japanese accessories and flower arrangements.

Western flower arrangers are not limited in the selection of suitable flower receptacles for their designs. Unconventional objects never intended for flowers are frequently employed to carry out a distinctive idea. Coffee pots, soup tureens and cooking utensils are some of the most popular. A piece of frosted glass, specially cut, makes a very lovely plaque for an arrangement of fruits done in our Western way. (Plate 23.) An old newel post that I found in a secondhand lumber yard produced three very interestingly shaped vases when cut in sections. (Plate 24.) The solid wood was scooped out to accommodate a metal lining.

In Japan I found many ingenious shapes and styles of receptacles used for flowers, but generally the styles were dictated by the school that advocated the traditional style of container. The exception is displayed in the modern schools and the modern adaptation in the classical schools of *ikebana*. I am grateful for the art I have learned from the Japanese people. I can feel its influence whenever I arrange flowers and wherever I see flowers arranged in the United States. (Plate 25.)

CHAPTER XII

Memo to My American Friends: Shopping and Eating in Tokyo

Although I was busy from early morning to late afternoon every day with my studies, the experiences I had in between lesson times were the ones I treasure most. I recall trips to the Ginza, the Tokyo shopping district, where I got lost on many occasions trying to find small specialty shops. The streets are not named or numbered, and unless you are familiar with Japanese calligraphy, they would be impossible to read anyway. The few phrases and words that I could speak in Japanese were not enough to communicate with the shop keepers.

Tokyo department stores were amazing. Not only were they as large, if not larger, than any we have in New York City, but they were filled from roof to subbasement with a variety of merchandise impossible to equal. The roof of most Tokyo department stores is utilized as a play area for children, with swings, slides, merry-go-rounds and other play apparatus. The Japanese mother can leave her little ones well attended and happily playing while she goes about her shopping on the floors below.

An entire floor is given to the display and sale of kimonos and obis (the traditional kimono sash) of all qualities for all occasions, and for all ages. The wedding kimono, I learned, is usually black with beautiful designs either woven, dyed or embroidered into the silk. Wedding kimonos are very costly by either Eastern or Western standards and often are resold after their initial wearing. There are a great variety of slightly worn kimonos for sale at a fraction of their original cost in a special basement department. In this same basement were wonderful antiques and slightly used furniture. I found charming *ikebana* baskets (Chap. 8), tables, stands, *kakemonos*, flower vases, and other art objects.

On another basement level food was sold. Baked goods, sweets, fruits, fish, meats, and delicatessen were temptingly displayed there. There was a restaurant for the convenience of the shopper. At the entrance to the restaurant there were showcases filled with prepared food in dishes with a number attached. The number helped in ordering your meal. This practical custom seemed to prevail in all Japanese restaurants where food is displayed in the street window.

An attractive Japanese member of the Tokyo chapter of the Ikebana International Society assisted me as an interpreter. We also had many good times together as she introduced me to delicious Japanese foods and wonderful out-of-the-way eating places I could have never discovered for myself. I was particularly enthusiastic about the *osushi* (raw fish) that is prepared in many different ways. It is really a delicacy. Wafer-thin slices of fresh, sweet raw fish fillets are wrapped around rice and seasoned with grated fresh ginger root, sweetened soy sauce, and other flavorful ingredients that vary with the kind of fish.

There was a special shop known for a hearty chicken and noodle dish called *gomoku*, made with vegetables. We slipped into this tiny eating place on a cool, rainy October evening. It was a memorable treat. Another specialty called *yukitori* was served in a miniature eating place that I am afraid I would have trouble finding again. *Yukitori* means "barbecue," the specialty of the house. There was a barbecue pit behind the counter where fragrant pieces of duck, beef, quail eggs, chicken livers, chicken, and shrimp were roasting, later to be served on small wooden skewers with rice and tea. The chef brushed the roasting foods with a sauce that I am sure is the secret of their special deliciousness. I went to Japan to study *ikebana*, but I came home with almost as many notes on Japanese cookery.

One of my most memorable after-lesson treats occurred on the day I shopped for my Japanese kimono. One of my Japanese friends escorted me to her kimono maker. The proprietress served tea before we started selecting the fabrics. We were seated on small stools around an elevated *tatami* platform while roll after roll of silk was brought out for our inspection. There was silk with designs woven into the fabric, silk in all colors, silk for dyeing, and silk of heavy, medium, and light weight. I selected a lightweight silk that was sent to Kyoto to be dyed a very pretty *café au lait*. It was difficult to select the silk for the obi. One was more beautiful than the next. Fine obi silks are hand-woven with gold and silver threads. My Sogetsu *sensei* invited me to an obi fashion show where only obi fabrics were displayed, one afternoon.

At first I did not understand about propriety in regard to selecting the color of my kimono. Tactfully I was told that "middle-aged ladies" wear somber colors. The young Japanese girl may wear gay, high shades with lots of design. (Plate 2.) I finally selected a rust-colored obi, with gold and silver maple leaves woven in it. My Japanese friend suggested that gold leaves be embroidered and painted on my kimono on the shoulder and bottom of the skirt.

I did not understand that the style of the kimono and the details of how it is worn are traditional with the Japanese. I thought my kimono would be made to fit, with no fold under the obi. The fold and adjustment of the length of a Japanese kimono, with the many ties to secure it, is a part of the Japanese tradition. We selected the *zoris* (Japanese shoes) and *tabis* (Japanese socks) as well as the proper undergarments worn with a kimono. I found the kimono to be a very comfortable and flattering garment for a woman to wear.

Western people are apt to confuse the Chinese dress with the Japanese. The high-colored, sheath-type dress with slits on the sides is the costume native to China, not Japan. The Japanese men wear a kimono at home, not a mandarin coat as some Westerners imagine. The kimono designed for men is simple and fastened at the waist with a sash. It is usually black or gray in color, and when made of cotton called *yukata*.

Happi coats are not traditional Japanese kimonos. They are made mostly for tourist consumption and are copies of the designs worn by men in different professions, e.g., firemen and policemen.

Before I went to Japan I bought a black Japanese apron with white calligraphy on it and a fish design at the bottom. I was very proud of it and wore it for my flower-arrangement work. Before leaving for Japan I asked a Japanese neighbor to advise me on the proper clothing to take to Japan during the season when I planned to be there. I showed her my prized apron with the beautiful white calligraphy and the fish painted on it. She laughed and asked me if I knew what the inscription on my apron meant. I admitted I did not, and she said, "You are wearing the equivalent of an American advertisement. The inscription on your apron translated means, 'Fish flakes make the finest consommé.'" We had a good laugh when we realized how close I had come to taking the apron to Japan to wear in my flower-arrangement classes. I never would have known what the ladies were giggling at when I wore it. Needless to say, I left it at home.

Japanese silks have a particular character of their own. The kimono and obi silks are sold in special shops or departments. The Japanese printed and plain-colored silks are well worth buying. If you have time, the Japanese do fine dressmaking. Brocade silks are usually Chinese in origin, although there are some made in Japan that are a little different in texture and design.

Shopping for cultured pearls is part of the enjoyment of shopping in Japan. Unless you have the good fortune to be escorted to a special shop by a Japanese friend, it is best to buy in the fine, well-established pearl stores. It is usually the cheapest in the long run.

In Kyoto I saw beautiful lacquer ware being made. When you see the painstaking care and hours of labor that go into the execution of a single piece, it is easy to understand why it is costly.

No visitor to Japan can leave without wishing to own some of the lovely woodcuts and prints. In Kyoto there are studios where visitors are welcome. It is fascinating to see the ancient process still being carried on with such artistry.

Japan is a "one price" country. Most of the merchandise is marked and there is little room for bargaining as there may be in other parts of the world. The Japanese do not have their "hand out" for a tip. They are a proud people. Some taxi drivers even refused to take a tip when I offered it. It was a new experience for a woman from New York, and quite refreshing.

There is a beautiful relationship between children and parents in a Japanese family. It is the accepted custom for the child to revere his parents. It is also customary for the oldest son to look after his aging parents. When he marries it is understood that if his mother is widowed, she will live with the young couple. I was told that sometimes an unwise mother-in-law can make the new bride very unhappy and even destroy an otherwise good marriage, while a wiser woman makes life pleasant for the whole family.

It is impossible to skip the Japanese theater when you visit Japan. The Kabuki short plays are performed in groups, and, like our Shakespearean plays that are so well attended in the United States, are very popular in Japan. The translation of the story is printed in English in a special program for visitors. The Noh plays are not easy for the average Western visitor to appreciate, but are well worth a try. Western theater is very popular in Japan, especially the American movies. I had the good fortune to meet a very charming woman who was the head of a modern theater group. She directs Japanese players in Shakespearean as well as modern drama.

It is not uncommon to hear Western visitors to Japan say that Japan is a place they would like to return to. This is probably because a short stay is not enough to take in and enjoy all that Japan has to offer. Like the Japanese garden that purposely conceals beautiful little plants or partially conceals the beauty of a stone lantern, much that is beautiful and wonderful in Japan is not obvious at the first glance.

Glossary of Japanese Words

Cha-no-yu	(chah-nō-yoō)	*Tea Ceremony*
chaseki	(chah-sèkēē)	*teahouse*
chasen	(chah-sėn)	*bamboo whisk*
chashaku	(chah-shahk)	*green powdered tea*
cha-ire	(cha-eero)	*tea caddy*
chawan	(chah-wahn)	*tea bowl*
choowa	(chō-wah)	*harmony*
chukan	(choō-kawn)	*supporting branch in ikebana*
Enshu	(eǹ-shoo)	*name of ancient classical school of ikebana founded by Kobori Enshu*
fuku shi	(foō-koò-shee)	*name for secondary or Man branch in Ohara method*
futon	(foò-tawn)	*mattress*
gato kago	(gahtō kahgō)	*basket used for flowers*
gekko gata	(gĕk-kō gah-tàh)	*hanging flower receptacle in crescent-moon shape*
gomoku	(gō-mō-koō)	*special kind of chicken, vegetable, and noodle soup*
gyo	(gee-ò)	*name for branch also called Man in Enshu method*
Hakoji	(hah-kahjee)	*name of basket weaver*
heikwa	(hày-kah)	*name for flowers arranged in tall vase*
hidari	(hǐ-dahrēē)	*left side*
hikae	(hi-kǐee)	*name for branch also known as Earth in Sogetsu method*
ikebana	(eeke-bahnah)	*flower arrangement*
Ikenobo	(eeken-ōbō)	*the oldest school of flower art in Japan*
jaku	(jahk)	*tranquillity*
jun-karo	(joōn kahrō)	*junior council for the Ikenobo school of teachers*

kago	(kahgō)	*woven basket used for flowers*
kake banaike	(kahkǎ bah-naēēke)	*wall basket*
karo	(kahrò)	*council of flower masters in the Ikenobo school*
kei	(kay)	*reverence*
kenzan	(kèn-zahn)	*needle-point flower holder*
Kinkakuji	(kēēnkahkōōjēē)	*Golden Pavilion, Kyoto, Japan*
kincoo	(kēēn-kō)	*balance applying to art*
kirei	(kee-ray)	*pretty*
koboshi	(kō-bō-shee)	*waste bowl*
koto	(kō-tō)	*Japanese musical instrument with a harplike tone*
kubari	(koo-bàhree)	*name for wooden flower holder*
kurikaeshi	(kūrēē-kī-eshee)	*repetition pertaining to art, e.g. repetition of color in a painting*
kwa bin	(kwah bēēn)	*flower vase*
Kwado-no-on-lamoto	(kwahdō-nō-ŏn-lahmōtō)	*Master of the Way of Flowers, honorary name given flower masters in the Ikenobo school*
kyaku-shi	(kẙǎ kōō shēē)	*branch or flower in Ohara method also called "object" and Earth*
mai	(mī-ēē)	*flowers or branches placed to support the main stems in ikebana*
Man-yo-shu	(Mahn yō shōō)	*book of ancient poetry*
migi	(mēē-ġēē)	*right side*
moribana	(morēē-bàhnah)	*shallow-dish style of flower arrangement*
nado	(nahdō)	*window*
nagashi	(nahgàh-shēē)	*name of branch in flower arrangement with flowing line in Enshu school also called Earth*
nageire	(nah-gày-eeray)	*throw-in style of flower arrangement*
niju-ike	(nēējōō ēēkĭ)	*two- or three-tier bamboo flower container*
Ohara	(Óhàh-rah)	*Master of Ohara school*
otoshi	(oh-tŏsh-ee)	*name given branch in Enshu school also known as Earth branch when the line is more modified*
rikkwa	(rēēk-kah)	*ancient style of ikebana*

Reshojo	(rōshō-jō)	*name of basket weaver*
sabi	(sahbee)	*quality of mellowness*
samurai	(sham-yoo-riee)	*Japanese warrior or swordsman*
san	(sahn)	*mister, madam, or miss*
sei	(say)	*purity of mind*
seikwa	(say-kah)	*style of flower arrangement in tall vase*
sensei	(sen-sày)	*teacher*
shin	(sheen)	*main branch, also called Heaven branch*
shoji	(sho-jee)	*sliding door made of strips of wood and rice paper*
shu shi	(shoo shee)	*Ohara school name of main branch in flower arrangement, also called "subject"*
soe	(soyee)	*name for Man branch in Ikenobo school*
Sogetsu	(sō-gets)	*name of modern flower-arrangement school in Tokyo*
suiban	(sooee-bahn)	*shallow-dish container for flowers originally used for sand garden*
sunabachi	(s'n-bahchee)	*shallow dish for flowers also used for miniature landscapes*
sungiri	(soon-jèe-ree)	*simple bamboo cylinder vase*
tabi	(tàhbee)	*special socks worn with Japanese sandals*
tai	(tiee)	*Ikenobo name for Earth branch*
tatami	(tahtàhmee)	*straw matting*
tobi ishi	(tobee eeshee)	*steppingstones in garden*
tokonoma	(tō-kō-nō-mă)	*shrinelike alcove found in Japanese home*
tomeki	(tō-màykee)	*extra piece of wood used to support stems with* kubari *holder in Ikenobo and other classical schools of ikebana*
tsuki gata	(tsookee-gahtah)	*hanging vase, crescent-moon shape*
tsukubai	(tsoo-koo-bī)	*stone water basin*
usubata	(oos-bah-tah)	*bronze flower container*
wa	(wah)	*harmony of mind*
wabi	(wah-bee)	*like* sabi *applied to person, e.g., a monk*
yukitori	(yù kee-tawree)	*barbecued food*
zori	(zàwree)	*Japanese sandals*

Bibliography

Anthology of Japanese Literature, Compiled by Donald Keene; Grove Press, New York, 1955

Architectural Beauty in Japan, Sutem Horiguchi; The Thomas Y. Crowell Co., New York, 1956

The Art of Flower Arrangement in Japan, A. L. Sadler; London Country Life, Ltd., 1955

The Art of Japanese Flower Arrangement, Alfred Koehn; J. L. Thompson & Co., Ltd., Japan, and Kegan Paul, Trench, Trubner & Co., Ltd., London, 1933

Art of the Landscape Garden in Japan, Tamura Tsuyoshi; Dodd, New York, 1936

The Book of Tea, Okakura Kakuso; Kenkyusha, Tokyo, 1951

Buddhism and Zen, Nyogen Senzaki and Ruth Strout McCandless; Philosophical Library, New York, 1953

A Confucian Notebook, Edward Herbert; Grove Press, New York, 1950

Form and Space of Japanese Architecture, Norman F. Carver; Charles Tuttle Company, Rutland, Vermont and Tokyo, 1956

Gardens of Japan, Jiro Harada; Studio Ltd., London, 1928

Gardens of Japan, Gisei Takakawa; Charles E. Tuttle Company, Rutland, Vermont and Tokyo, 1958

History of Religions, George Foote Moore, D.D., LLD., Litt. D.; Charles Scribner's Sons, New York, 1929

Ikenobo School of Japanese Floral Art, Edited by Tsutomu Nishimura; Ikenobo Floral Art Institute, Kyoto, Japan, 1951.

Japanese Gardens, Matsumotsue Tatsui, Charles E. Tuttle Company, Rutland, Vermont and Tokyo, 1953

Japanese Gardens of Today, David H. Engel; Charles E. Tuttle Company, Rutland, Vermont and Tokyo, 1959

Japanese Temples and Tea Houses, Werner Blaser; F. W. Dodge Corporation, New York, 1957

Japanese Traditional Gardens, Yoshuobu Yoshinaja; Charles E. Tuttle Company, Rutland, Vermont and Tokyo

The Mastery of Japanese Flower Arrangement, Busho Juga ku and Keichii Fujii; Kyu Soga Gosho Kwado Soshicho, Kyoto, Japan, 1940

Nippon No Tsien (Gardens of Japan); Charles E. Tuttle Company, Rutland, Vermont and Tokyo

Observations on Japanese Architecture, S. Horiguchi

One Thousand Years of Japanese Gardens, Tokyo News Service, Eno; Charles E. Tuttle Company, Rutland, Vermont and Tokyo, 1955

The Path of Light, a Manual of Mahayana Buddhism, L. D. Barnett, Litt. D., M.A.; John Murray, London, 1954

Some Old Kyoto Gardens and Their Thought, Charles Hitchcock Sherrill; Kokusai Bunka Shinkokai, Kyoto, Japan, 1933–37

Tao Te Ching (The Book of the Way and the Virtues), tr. from the Chinese by J. J. L. Duydendak; John Murray, London, 1954

Tea Cult of Japan, Fukukita Yasunosuke; Vol. 4, Japan Travel Bureau Tourist Library, 1947

The Theory of Japanese Flower Arrangements, Josiah Conder; Published with permission of Asiatic Society of Japan, by Empire State Book Co., New York, 1936

Zen and Fine Art, Hisamatsu, Hoseki, Shinichi; Bokubi-Sha, Kyoto, 1958

Zen and Japanese Cultures, D. T. Suzuki; Pantheon Books, Inc., New York, 1959

Index